The Intermediate Cellist

MILLY B. STANFIELD

LONDON
OXFORD UNIVERSITY PRESS
1973

Oxford University Press, Ely House, London W.1

GLASGOW NEW YORK TORONTO MELBOURNE WELLINGTON
CAPE TOWN IBADAN NAIROBI DAR ES SALAAM LUSAKA ADDIS ABABA
DELHI BOMBAY CALCUTTA MADRAS KARACHI LAHORE DACCA
KUALA LUMPUR SINGAPORE HONG KONG TOKYO

ISBN 0 19 318508 3

Printed in Great Britain
by Ebenezer Baylis & Son Limited
The Trinity Press, Worcester, and London

TO MAURICE EISENBERG

in deep appreciation of the wisdom and knowledge revealed in his teaching and through the example of his artistry

ACKNOWLEDGEMENTS

ACKNOWLEDGEMENTS and thanks are due to Eric Lavender, Editor of *The Strad*, for his kind permission to use material originally written for his journal;

to the generosity of Maurice Eisenberg and Novello and Co Ltd for allowing quotations, both musical and verbal, from Mr Eisenberg's technique book: *Cello Playing of Today*;

and, on a different level, to the writer's many pupils of all ages and many nationalities who unconsciously provided such a revealing insight into the problems of cellists in embryo.

Most particularly, however, must the deepest appreciation be expressed to Maurice Eisenberg for his help and kindness in reading the script, offering suggestions to make it more complete, and permitting the use of a number of his exercises evolved over the last few years, which are quoted in the later chapters. His sudden death on 13 December 1972, while teaching at the Juilliard School, New York, robbed the cello world of one of its most outstanding figures.

MILLY B. STANFIELD

CONTENTS

PART IV PIZZICATO FOR CELLISTS

PART V REFLECTIONS AND REMINDERS

GLOSSARY OF SIGNS USED

⊓ = down bow

V = up bow

l.h. pizz. = sound the notes only through the percussion of the fingers of the left hand

s = semitone

x = extension

xx = double extension

⌐¬ = groups of notes in the same position or groups of notes to be considered in relation to each other

I = the A string

II = the D string

III = the G string

IV = the C string

L_J = keeping a finger on the string while playing other notes

, = breathing place in the music, equivalent to a comma

Q = use the left thumb to play a note or notes

(Q) = prepare the left thumb across the strings ready to play in the thumb position

(.) = open string which can be used to test the intonation when practising or a note on which a finger can be placed before articulating a higher note on the same string

FOREWORD

by

MAURICE EISENBERG

I FEEL proud and honoured that Milly Stanfield has dedicated *The Intermediate Cellist* to me.

When she came to study with me in Paris in the 1930s and attended my classes at the École Normale de Musique as a regular listener she made notes of my comments and let me read them. I recognized then and there her unique talent for getting to the heart of the most complicated technical matters and putting them into simple words and phrases, expressed so clearly that they could be readily understood by any player. She has now enjoyed over many years a large following of enthusiastic readers in many parts of the world who have followed her contributions to *The Strad* with much benefit.

The elementary logical truths of technique can never be stressed often enough. No one can deny the tremendous difficulty of playing the cello and the enormous problems attached to producing a good tone, controlling the bowing, strengthening the left hand, individualizing the work of each finger, synchronizing the movements of both hands and arms, achieving command of the intonation and a varied vibrato. Then there is the smooth crossing of the strings, the shifting of position, the distribution of the bow, breathing and punctuation, posture and all it implies.

Teacher-performers find it natural to illustrate to their pupils the fruits of their experiences, 'for what they play is what they are'. However, students and amateurs need the ready dictionary of uncomplicated terminology to help them when they are on their own. They will find authoritative answers here to many questions that crop up during their daily practising which will open their eyes and ears when pursuing their quest for improvement.

The Intermediate Cellist also delves into the human and psychological problems, such as the avoidance of mannerisms, 'trac' control, recurrent weaknesses, and, perhaps above all, how to practise intelligently. In focusing attention on these elements which are constantly with them, this book should be of invaluable assistance in aiding students to avoid or overcome many difficulties and make their practising more enjoyable and beneficial.

I heartily recommend this excellent work to all cellists of all ages and categories who wish to analyse their weaknesses and improve their standard of playing.

May 1972

INTRODUCTION

Many cellists over the years have asked me to publish excerpts of my *Strad* articles in book form. Until recently, the answer was always: 'Well, perhaps one day!' There was no leisure for such an undertaking while working full time as Administrative Secretary and assistant teacher to Maurice Eisenberg at the International Cello Centre in London. Since leaving England, however, this restriction no longer applies, and when the New York music publisher and cello enthusiast, Alexander Broude, made the same suggestion I was encouraged to give the idea serious consideration.

My first technique article, written during my Paris student days, appeared on 1 January 1938. The editorial directive was to contribute a thousand words a month in a series specifically suited to cellists of moderate ability. With this in mind I was to elucidate the principles underlying the Pablo Casals school of cello playing.

At that time this project represented a big step forward. The pedagogic field in the English-speaking countries was still mainly dominated, directly or indirectly, by the influence of the nineteenth-century virtuoso cellists from Central Europe. Casals's art, with its profundity, beauty, and illusion of ease, was regarded by the majority of his co-instrumentalists as a law unto itself. Even after the publication in 1919 of Diran Alexanien's treatise, *The Technique of the Violoncello*, with its illuminating analysis of the Casals innovations, most of his contemporaries considered its novel ideas as being solely applicable to the élite.

Perhaps this was understandable. The Catalan master was immersed in his concert activities. For three decades his teaching had been virtually restricted to a few chosen artist-pupils, notably Guilhermina Suggia in the early years of his career, Gaspar Cassado as a young student in Barcelona, and Maurice Eisenberg from 1929 until the outbreak of the Spanish Civil War at his summer home, San Salvador. Otherwise during the greater part of the inter-war period practically his only personal link with cellists of the future came through the Pablo Casals Class at the École Normale de Musique in Paris. As its Director, he heard the students regularly for several years, and his technical and interpretative precepts provided the basis of its teaching, first under Alexanien and later under Eisenberg. It was not until Casals had left Spain and, as an anti-Dictatorship protest, cancelled his concert tours that he began accepting pupils at Prades and started giving Master Classes in Zermatt, California, and Puerto Rico. At 96 he still visits the Serkin School at Marlboro, Vermont, in this latter capacity, and conducts its orchestra of young professionals.

His example has undoubtedly popularized the cello as a solo instrument. The number of players has increased enormously since his first appearance and the average standard of performance has become far higher as the effects of his reforms are being assimilated. His former pupils now occupy key posts in many countries, attracting knowledgeable students and audiences. Moreover Eisenberg's 1957 book, *Cello Playing of Today* (Lavender Publications, Novello's, London), which is now in its second edition has familiarized countless performers and students with the logic behind every detail of Casals's cellistic ideology, whether it is applied in the classics or as a background to modernity.

In the meantime, the century moves onwards. New personalities are emerging, each with a slightly different point of view. Contemporary composers make ever growing demands on instrumentalists and fresh idioms often require manipulative action that would have seemed incredible a decade or two ago. In order to keep abreast with the pace of the times serious students have to adapt their whole attitude towards practising, training themselves to be more selective in the material they use so that they can cover the ground faster. The problem lies in accomplishing this without sacrificing the quality essential to the style, technique, and interpretation.

Despite these developments, regardless of much gratifying improvement, the fundamental laws of fine cello playing do not change. There remains a persistent need for complete understanding of the basic elementary precepts at all times. Advanced books and études by distinguished artist-professors can be invaluable, but numerous players—some amateur, some in a relatively early stage of studentship, some second-study teachers—require specialized advice of a simpler kind.

These 'intermediate cellists' are often hampered by lack of sufficient time at the instrument; they may live in an area where it is difficult to get good lessons; they may need frequent reminders concerning the incidence of inherent weaknesses as well as a spur to progress. It is for this large and varied group that these pages have been compiled. Some of the subject matter has been slightly edited to avoid unnecessary repetition but certain factors have had to be treated recurrently because they affect different issues. In choosing what to include there has been only one objective, although adherence to it has meant omitting coverage of many interesting events and interviews with prominent personalities: to bring out points and issues that might prove of direct help to readers in furthering their cellistic attainments in the future.

PART ONE

Some Problems of Cello Playing

BASIC PRINCIPLES: POSITION AT THE INSTRUMENT

AMONG THE many musical evolutions witnessed during the present century few have been more striking than the growing popularity of the violoncello as a solo instrument. During the greater part of the eighteen-hundreds solo playing was chiefly confined to a few outstanding virtuosi, such as Romberg, Davidoff, Popper and Piatti. These and certain of their followers did much to build up constructive schools of cellistic thought. Nevertheless, it was only with the emergence of Pablo Casals that the majority of music lovers became aware of the supreme beauty that could be produced from this somewhat cumbersome instrument. In his hands the most exacting concerto or unaccompanied suite appeared comparatively simple, the expression of a musical ideology rather than the execution of a series of technical feats. Small wonder that encouraged by his example musicians came to regard the cello in a new light and studied it with an entirely different outlook.

In actual fact, the seeming ease which has always been so notable a feature of Casals's art is sadly deceptive, being the result of his phenomenal interpretative vision and instrumental talent coupled with years of profound thought and careful preparation. The instrument remains—and will probably always remain—one of exceptional difficulty, bringing problems that can only be solved after much intelligent work. During recent decades, however, such progress has been made towards their elucidation that the possibility of successful performance has been brought to many who might formerly have been content to play a few bass notes in the family band.

Foremost of the initial problems confronting students is

the question of balance. This involves the distribution of weight between the hands, the development of muscular freedom and the training of each hand to play its part in sympathy with the other but without being unduly influenced by it. If these fundamental principles are mastered early in studentship players may subsequently be spared the vexatious task of correcting defects that need never have come into being. For example, how many cellists have become muscle-bound by forcing the tone through crouching over the instrument and pressing down on the bow, often accompanying this with facial and bodily contortions which defeat the performer's object by squashing the tone inwards instead of letting it out? This is a common instance of faulty balance.

The position of the player at the instrument is of great importance here. Sitting upright like a good rider, the back straight but never rigid, shoulders squared and feet planted firmly on the ground, is not only to be advocated from an aesthetic point of view. It gives suppleness and freedom to the whole system and allows liberty of action to the muscles behind the shoulder-blades which control the arms and hands.

On the cello the muscles of the back and arms are used in much the same way as in archery. Beginners, therefore, may find it helpful to sit at the instrument for a few moments from time to time with both hands raised as if shooting an imaginary arrow (but with the right arm outstretched instead of the left) in order to grow accustomed to the sensation of pulling *back* against the left shoulder while pulling *out* with the bow arm.

The cello should always be at the best possible height for the player. The end-pin should be carefully adjusted to the build of the individual performer and adapted, when necessary, to suit each chair. Its length can generally be determined by the position of the left hand in the first position, where the index finger should be almost opposite the shoulder.

If correct, this placement will enable the arm weight to pass unhindered into the fingers. To help it become instinctive, elementary students should grasp the neck of the cello with the whole hand at first position level and pull back as if strap-hanging. *The lower arm and the elbow should be in a straight line with the hand.* To extend the benefits of this drill to the establishment of a feeling of co-ordination with the right hand, the bow should be placed on the string at the point on full hair. Pull forward with the right arm and back with the left, hold this position briefly and then relax both arms.

The bow arm should be free, its movements devoid of either stiffness or floppiness. At the outset it might be considered as a pendulum that swings in and out from the shoulder socket. Later, players should find that their natural intensity can pass freely down the arm unit through the elbow and wrist into the fingers to be transmitted on to the bow by means of the sensitive pressure of the finger tips against the thumb on the 'frog'. This is vital to the creation of a fine tone.

To put these precepts into practice, work sustained notes near the bridge. Start at the nut on about three-quarters of the hair, the wrist high and the bow held firmly in the hand. The stick should be turned gradually in the fingers as it is pulled out so that full hair is reached at the tip, their action being reversed on the up bows. The tone should be of maximum strength without scratchiness. If the same quantity and quality are to be maintained it will be found that it is necessary to bow somewhat quicker in the upper—and lighter—half of the bow and to increase the pressure of the fingers on the stick as the point is neared. The following exercise should be useful. The whole length of the bow should be used on every note and a uniform tone preserved throughout.[1]

BOW CONTROL

A thorough command of the bow may demand the use of every joint and muscle from the hips to the finger tips. Thus the art of bowing freely and smoothly usually requires much patient study. With careful training, however, good bowing can be developed gradually and logically. Eventually it should become as instinctive to the performer as a controlled breast stroke is to a strong swimmer.

The primary difficulties are generally concerned with the regulation of the arm movement. The arm might be compared to a door which opens and shuts, and the ball-bearing joints—that is to say the shoulder socket, elbow and wrist—to the hinges. Except in rare cases the latter are all used whenever the bow is pulled over the strings yet the 'door', i.e. the whole arm unit, should move in one piece.

The co-ordination of action between the shoulder and the hand is complicated by the fact that the various parts of the arm often have to move at different speeds. If the distance from the wrist to the bridge is measured when the bow is at the point it will be found to be about three times greater than it is between the elbow and the side of the cello. This means

[1] Other variations of this drill and those quoted on the following page will be found in Chapter III of Eisenberg's *Cello Playing of Today*.

that the lower arm has to travel roughly three times faster than the upper arm.

Exercises such as:

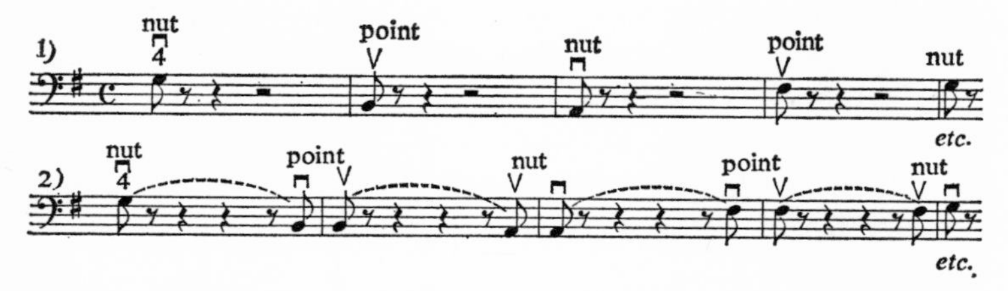

which involve playing alternately at either extremity of the bow should be practised daily to develop the correct reflexes. Give little bow on the actual notes, and continuing the stroke without altering its speed, carry the bow above the string in the rests as if playing on an imaginary fifth string placed over the others. Every time the nut is neared a conscious effort should be made to raise the wrist and acquire a feeling of 'coming home' in the muscles behind the shoulder blade. In the second exercise the changes of bow should be accomplished by an almost imperceptible sideways movement of the fingers on the 'frog'.

The muscles can likewise be trained to accustom themselves to the necessary adjustments by a silent drill. Place the bow on the string at the point and grip the tip firmly with the *left* hand to keep the stick in position, horizontal to the bridge. Hold the right hand loosely over the stick with the fingers hanging down on its farther side and the thumb on its nearer side. Then slide the hand backwards and forwards along the wood. The fingers should lead the way when pulling out and the wrist when pushing in.

A change of string must never be allowed to affect the arm movement, which should be from side to side, not up and down. The bow should follow the line of the bridge and cross the strings at right angles. The trouble is that the top of the bridge is curved instead of being straight. Therefore, while it is comparatively easy to keep the bow parallel with the bridge on the middle strings when sitting squarely at the cello, it is almost impossible to do so when playing on the A or the C if the body remains in exactly the same position.

This difficulty can be overcome by an infinitessimal swing of the trunk of the body from the hips upwards. Those to whom this idea is new should remember that the instrument, as the cellist's 'centre of gravity', should remain more or less immovable, firmly gripped between the knees, and that the set of the shoulders and balance of weight in both arms are also established factors which must never be disturbed. If the height of the arm were to be changed whenever it was necessary to play on a different string it would interfere with the smoothness of the bowing and so prove detrimental to the tone. However, equal freedom and control *must* be maintained on all the strings, so the solution lies in adjusting the upper part of the body in proportion to the minute changes in string-level occasioned by the rounding of the bridge.

In quick passages one often has to cross the strings so rapidly that there is no time for this action, but the same idea can be carried out in miniature by the wrist and fingers. The degree of their movement depends on the speed of the passages concerned. To prepare the fingers, over-string arpeggio exercises should be worked.

A variety of these can be found in Grützmacher's *Daily Studies*. To begin with, however, one can hardly do better than place the bow on the C string at the nut, rest the elbow on the 'ribbing' of the cello and play an open chord up and down over the four strings:

only using as much bow as is needed to give full play to the fingers and wrist. Later, experiment with the opening lines of the Prelude of Bach's solo suite in G. Take each bar slowly, four notes to a bow, and treat it as an exercise. Start with the bow poised as if playing on the D string and reach down and up respectively to play the notes on the G and A strings by adjusting the pressure and angle of the fingers on the nut. Listen critically and plan the bow distribution to ensure, as far as possible, that there is uniformity of tone throughout.

FINGER PERCUSSION AND FINGER PLACING

Few who have listened to any of the world's great string players at close range in a concert hall can have failed to notice that the percussion of the fingers on the string can be heard clearly in the auditorium. Even in passages where from a distance the chief interest lies apparently in the bowing, near to it is often discovered that the left hand is master of the situation. Obviously, strong, flexible finger action is essential to the foundation of a sound technique.

As a preparatory step students should devote a certain amount of time to practising exercises for the left hand without using the bow. Begin by placing the hand ready to play in the first position on the C string. The thumb should be under the neck of the cello opposite the E♭, the rounded fingers close to each other and raised high above the string like a broad crook. They should all descend to help the first finger pluck the open string C and raise themselves again without any break in the hand movement. Next drop the index finger on to the D as if sinking right into the finger-board, backed by the concentrated weight of the whole arm as well as that of the hand unit. Then, always keeping the finger firmly on the note and the thumb behind the neck, lift the back of the hand and the remaining fingers as high as possible so that the second finger is ready to fall on to the E♭ in a similar way. When this note has been enunciated, adopt the same procedure for the third finger on E♮ and the fourth finger on F.

After the F has been reached and the four fingers are on their notes, start descending by lifting the fingers one by one with a plucking movement, simultaneously pulling back very slightly with the elbow. This gives out the sound of the held note immediately below it: that is to say when the fourth finger in the afore-quoted drill is plucked the E will be heard and so on. The exercise should be worked slowly, counting four in every bar, so that each finger can be prepared in advance. Only thus will the maximum benefit be gained from such drills. At first it may be difficult to produce a clear sound, especially with the third and fourth fingers, but with practice they will soon gain strength.

This approach can be adapted to scales, arpeggios, finger exercises (other than double-stopping) and even pieces. If intelligently applied it can have far-reaching results. It makes the fingers strong and supple, giving them flexibility and independence, while the arm weight, used as a natural asset, helps players to reach the heart of each note. Furthermore, providing that the fingers are well placed it enables the hand to shape itself in a way which will eventually add to the security of the intonation. In addition, it gives cellists a chance of acquiring, almost subconsciously, the habit of using left-hand pizzicato to mitigate against any change in tonal texture when passing from a stopped note to an open string in bowed passages.

When the playing length of a string is shortened by a stopped note it vibrates differently to when it is at its full playing length on an open string. It tends to respond slower when set in motion solely by the stroke of the bow, consequently the sound is apt to be fractionally delayed on an open string. To compensate for this discrepancy the open string should be plucked by a finger of the left hand at the exact moment that it is struck by the bow. To prove the effectiveness of this procedure play the first octave of G major scale both with and without a slight left hand pizzicato on the D, listening intently. The difference will be particularly evident when ascending where the string is shortened to a quarter of its maximum length by the fourth finger on C immediately before the open string D.

The 'placing' of the fingers, to which passing reference has already been made, is extremely important because of its influence on the intonation. The need for it will be realized by experimenting in the first two octaves of C minor scale, melodic form, ascending:[1]

where the whole tones and semitones occur on different places on every string. This virtually forces the hand to adopt a specific 'placing' on each group of four notes.

Bar I. The fingers play a minor third which contains first a semitone and then a whole tone. The hand must be 'square' with the fingerboard in order to allow enough space for the

[1] Also quoted in *Cello Playing of Today* by Maurice Eisenberg.

whole tone to be stretched between the second and the fourth fingers. Otherwise, as the little finger is so short, the F tends to be flat.

Bar II. The fingers again cover a minor third but this time the whole tone falls between the first and third fingers and the sensitive semitone from the leading note to the tonic, between the third and fourth. If the hand remained in 'squared placing' as in bar I, most probably either the third finger would be flat or the fourth finger sharp. However, by imperceptibly turning the hand unit to 'side placing' in which the fingers point downwards towards the bridge, their natural position will bring the third and fourth fingers into the correct placing on both notes.

Bar III. Here two whole tones lie between the first and fourth fingers. This involves a 'squared' hand placing and a backward extension with the first finger. The second must be in the middle of the hand, at right angles to the string while the first points away from it towards the head of the cello.

Bar IV. This contains a minor third with a whole tone between the open string A and the first finger B. The latter being the leading note should be as near the tonic C as possible. The fingers playing this semitone will be closer together if both point slightly downwards, thus determining the hand placing.

These bars form a useful key from which to work out placings in other scales and passages. When studied methodically the results should be most rewarding, leading ultimately to the development of an organized hand, ready to play in tune with certainty and accuracy.

INDEPENDENCE OF THE ARMS

The development of independence of movement in both

arms *simultaneously* is apt to cause inexperienced players considerable trouble. The fingers and bow have to perform such different functions that although they are bound to influence each other to some extent the hands frequently seem to be employed in opposite ways. It is really necessary to acquire a dual sense of concentration so that, for instance, when playing a passage involving jumps and stretches for the left hand one never loses sight of the importance of bow control, or when striving to execute complicated bowings, fails to pay attention to maintaining strength and flexibility in the fingers of the left hand.

There are two good methods of training the hands to become independent of each other while preserving a sense of co-ordination. One is to work at studies: Lee, Dotzauer, Piatti, Franchomme, Popper, for example, or the well chosen anthology contained in Joachim Stutschewsky's six-volume collection of études. These provide players with the opportunity of accomplishing a series of carefully graded technical feats with *both* hands which enables them to develop disciplined freedom of action in a natural way.

The second approach consists of practising scales and arpeggios with a variety of bowings and rhythms. This is particularly useful to those who have only a limited amount of time to spend at the instrument. It is simple yet challenging and students will find that as they grow more proficient they can invent variations for themselves founded on the problems encountered in their solo and ensemble work.

Start by practising a scale slowly, two notes (a minim or a half-note each) to a bow. Next, the same scale should be played with four notes (crotchets or quarter-notes) and subsequently eight notes (quavers or eighth-notes) to a bow. Listen to the tone which should be full and clear in all registers, and to the intonation, remembering the help that can be derived from the finger placing. (See pp. 11–12.)

Also work them with short separate strokes towards the centre of the bow in three different ways: legato, on-the-string detaché, and a controlled spiccato. First repeat each note four times, then three times, and then twice, before finally attempting the scale in single notes. Be careful to use the same amount of bow on every note and make sure that the tone quality does not vary. When these bowings are on the right road, the following should be added:

Another series of drills can be made up by playing the scale entirely at the nut or the point. Use only as much bow as is needed to allow the fingers and wrist to change bow freely. Some suggested bowings are:

which can likewise be worked starting up bow. The last two variations applied legato four and eight notes to a bow, also form a useful exercise for the left hand.

More advanced cellists should play a two- or four-octave scale three times without stopping, *three* notes to a bow. This brings the accent on to a fresh note every time and adds to the independence of the fingers by forcing the player out of a possible groove. To terminate daily scale practice all students should try to perform their scale of the day fairly rapidly, two, three, or four octaves to a bow.

Arpeggios lend themselves to similar treatment but are

rather more difficult because of the awkwardness involved in keeping the fingers 'placed' while shifting the whole hand to and from a higher position. Take a three-octave arpeggio, three notes in a bow, and practise it first in its major and then in its minor form:

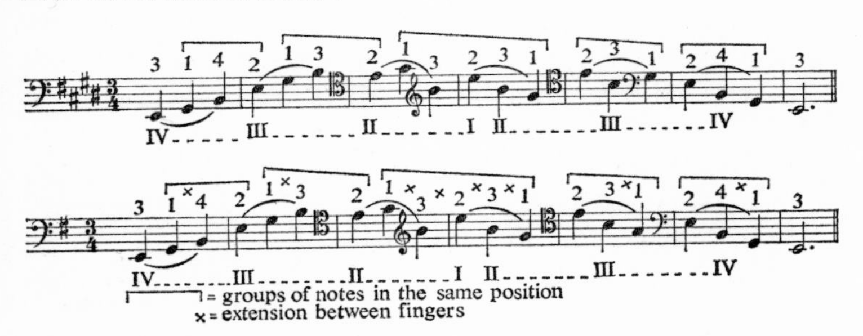

Each brings its own problems although the fingerings are identical. In the major, the principle difficulty consists of keeping the first and second fingers sufficiently close together while providing enough space for the whole tone stretch between the fingers in the lower part of the hand. Unless this is effected, the tonic (played by the second finger) tends to be sharp and the dominant (third or fourth finger, according to the octave) to be flat. In the minor there are stretches of a major third from the first to the fourth or the third fingers: thus the second finger has to be squarely in the middle of the hand and the first finger extended backwards, away from it. (See p. 12.) This brings the hand into an uncomfortable position for the slide from the second to the first finger when ascending which, unless guarded against by careful practising, will mar the tone on the index finger.

Although independence of action in each arm is essential if technical freedom is to be attained, there are many occasions when smudges occur because the timing of their movements fail to synchronize. In general the change of bow should coincide absolutely with the change of finger. To prevent blemishes due to lapses in this respect players should listen critically *between* the notes. They should seek, ultimately, to develop a sensation of extreme sensitivity, like a spark of electricity, in the finger tips of both hands.

The more vital the fingerwork becomes, the easier it should be for students to hear themselves. They should therefore add trill exercises to their 'daily dozen' at a relatively early stage in their instrumental life. Begin as if practising mordents, holding the first finger very firmly on the basic note and coming down as rapidly as possible with the second (and, if applicable, the third) which should be raised again immediately that the higher note has been struck. Continue with double mordents, and gradually increase the number of notes in the 'shake' until a whole trill is played. These ideas should also be applied to inverted trills starting from above, and eventually to all positions on all strings with every conceivable variety of fingering.

VIBRATO

Vibrato to a string player is like colour to a painter and in its relation to musical interpretation it often requires as much thought and care as the blending of tints and hues in oils and water colours. True, from an idealistic point of view it might be claimed that vibrato is a spontaneous reaction, the subconscious reflection of a performer's musical feeling. There are, indeed, a fortunate few who possess a special talent that enables them to vary the vibrations instinctively as the spirit of the music demands. But such cases are rare even among celebrated artists. Monotony of tone-colour is a criticism that may justly be levelled at many fine executants, and upon analysis it will generally be found that the fault, technically speaking, lies in a lack of variety in the texture and speed of the finger oscillations.

Not infrequently less gifted players are hampered in their efforts at self expression by a kind of inhibition. Before they can vibrate naturally they usually have to develop more flexibility in the hand and fingers. The left-hand pizzicato exercises (see pp. 9 and 10) should be of benefit here, especially if worked with the specific object of bringing the weight of the whole arm, without stiffening it, to the aid of whichever finger is momentarily in use.

It should be realized from the outset that in vibrato the hand should be supple but never flaccid. Beginners should start to develop it by moving the lower arm, wrist, and hand a short distance backwards and forwards over and parallel to the strings, the rounded fingers curled over the thumb. The whole unit should be kept in one piece from the elbow to the invisible finger tips, its motions becoming smaller and quicker. Next open the fist and transfer the oscillations in a yet more compact form to the cello, keeping the fingers grouped together. The cushion of the finger playing the note should remain in constant contact with the string, pressing it to the fingerboard. The thumb should be placed loosely under the neck: facing the 'home' of the second finger.

A good vibrato exercise can be made up by working a series of simple notes such as:

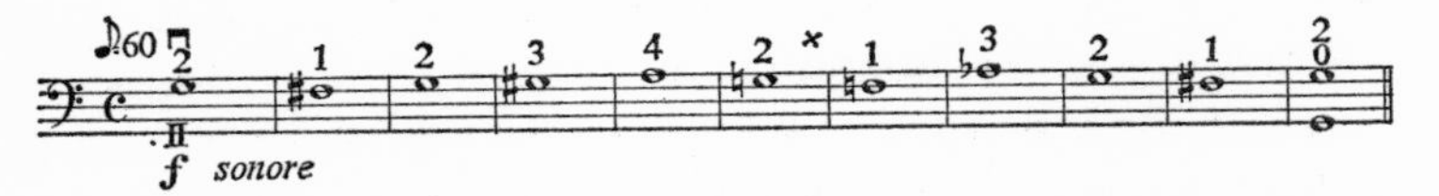

Aim at preserving the same quality of tone and a uniform speed of vibrato. Begin by playing each note with separate bows as indicated above. Follow this by slurring two or three notes in a bow, playing them twice as fast. At first it may be advisable to count a regular number of vibrations on every beat to make sure that the oscillations are under control. In general, however, the student should try to hear and feel, rather than rely on mathematical calculations in this branch of technique. The vibrations on one note should sink into those on the next: there must be no break in the tonal continuity when changing fingers or between bows.

Next, imagine that there is a sforzando on each note:

This means that a large, quick vibrato given at the commencement of every note should gradually subside into a smaller, slower movement and end in none at all. The bow distribution should be planned on similar lines, the greater part of the stroke being used at the beginning on the accent and progressively less as the tone dies away. A variation of this consists of playing a few notes in the same bow with a slight accent on each. This provides practice in altering the speed of the oscillations without interfering with the smoothness of the bowing. A further vibrato drill involves working legato breves (i.e. counting sixteen slow quavers or eighth-notes on every note) with a long crescendo in each bar. This is exactly opposite, both in idea and execution, to the sforzando exercise. Start the notes *ppp* using very little or no vibration and the minimum amount of bow. Then slowly increase the tone to a *ff* through an intensified movement in the vibrato and a gradually letting out of the bow. On the down bows it is particularly important to save up the bow at the beginning of the stroke so that as much as possible is held in reserve for the last two quavers (eighth-notes) towards the point where the bow is lightest.

The exact speed and intensity of the vibrato can only be

determined by the taste and temperament of the performer. It is as personal a matter as the pulse rate. Vibrato is part and parcel of the phrasing and atmosphere and as such must never be allowed to stagnate. In certain slow pieces—the Tartini Adagio (arr. Hugo Becker), the first and third movements of the Eccles, Marcello F major, and Porpora sonatas, the opening and closing sections of Dvořák's *Waldesruhe*, for instance—the quiet gait of the music demands a serene, calm vibration. In moods of greater stress, the quickening pulse of the music (not necessarily reflected in a change of tempo) calls for an increased intensity in the movement of the oscillations. This not only occurs in rapid or light works where the character and style obviously indicate the need of a somewhat smaller, quicker vibrato: it also applies in slow pieces which involve a heightening or deepening of emotional significance, calling for consequent gradations in the texture of the tone. Typical examples appear in the middle part of *Waldesruhe* and the third phrase (bars 9 to 16) of the Fauré *Elégie*, while they abound in the big concertos and sonatas.

In ensemble and orchestral work it will be found that accompanying crotchets and quavers carry best when played with a rather quick and very vital vibration at the beginning of each note. Sustained basses, on the other hand, require a full, quiet movement. Pizzicato can be helped by a big, tense vibrato, the fingers sinking into their notes with particular firmness so that when necessary the tone can ring on long after the right hand has left the string.

INTONATION

Intonation is undoubtedly the most complex problem associated with cello playing. Owing to the size and compass of the instrument it presents even greater difficulties than on the violin or viola where, thanks to the smaller spacing between the intervals, it is easier to rectify a 'false' note by an imperceptible movement of the finger tip. On the cello the distances between the tones and semitones are much larger and they vary so greatly in the different registers that performers desiring to play as perfectly in tune as possible generally find they are obliged to consider the placing of the hand and fingers in practically every passage until they have built up a 'fingerboard sense' which is equivalent to 'keyboard sense' on the piano.

With this in mind the fingers should be trained from an early stage to find their way almost automatically to certain specific notes. These should become recognized as landmarks to be treated as signposts to other notes in the vicinity. Begin by playing E on the A string, first finger in the fourth position, several times at intervals whilst practising. To accustom the fingers to finding it without immediate previous contact with the string, the arm should be hanging down away from the fingerboard before trying to 'pitch' it. The hand should then be lifted up, its side rested on the cello, the thumb placed in the crook of the neck and the rounded finger on the string. Directly the note has been sounded it should be repeated as a harmonic to test its accuracy.

When the first finger can rely on finding the note, it should be pitched in a similar way with the second finger and afterwards the third. As this will bring the E into the third position, the side of the hand will have to be at least an inch above the body of the instrument. On most cellos, however, the second finger on the E will still be opposite the thumb if the latter remains in the crook, although when experimenting with the third finger, it will be found that the thumb should be rather nearer the head of the cello.

As soon as the fingers can pitch the E (and its equivalent

on the lower strings) without fumbling, the following exercise:

should be added. The bowing must be legato throughout. *The accents should come solely from the weight and percussion of the fingers falling on to the string.*[1]

The advantage attached to using this E as a landmark will be appreciated when first locating other notes in the third and fourth positions. For instance, it is comparatively easy to play D♯ (or E♭), F, F♯, or G correctly once the E is in place providing the cellist listens attentively to make sure that the notes are in tune with each other. To familiarize the hand and ear with the relative placing of each note players should work finger-patterns in the same position which include both chromatic intervals and every variety of simple extensions. Take, for example:

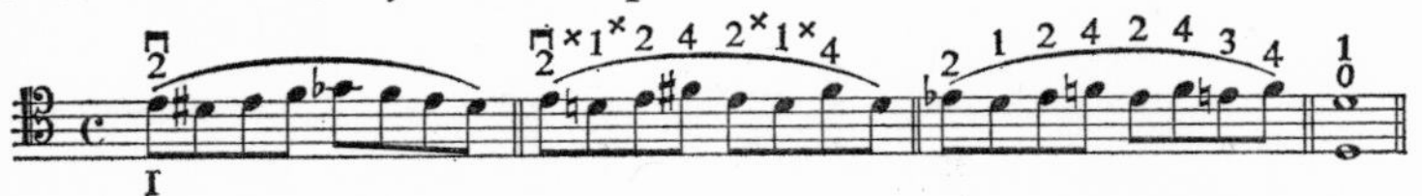

When starting to 'pitch' the second position difficulties are apt to increase because it is no longer possible to use the crook of the neck as a gauge. The D should be practised with the second finger as the E has been with the first, and tested as an octave over the open string. When this position is safely established other notes in the position can be added. Work drills like:

[1] Further drills on these lines and those similarly marked on pp. 21 and 50 will be found in *Cello Playing of Today* by Maurice Eisenberg.

on each set of strings in turn. The second finger should be in exactly the same place every time its note is repeated, which may be more difficult than is apparent at first sight. The second position can also be located through the index finger, considered in relationship to its familiar placement in the first position:

The harmonics above each open string are equally important as signposts for the positions of the middle register: the fifth to the seventh. Their position should be memorized in much the same way except that this time the procedure is reversed: the note should be sounded first as a harmonic and then repeated as a stopped note. Start with the third finger and wait until it can be pitched with certainty before using the second finger and finally the first. Subsequently an exercise on stopped As can be recommended:[1]

These suggestions should prove helpful in making the fingers feel at home in the various parts of the fingerboard in the lower and middle registers. Nevertheless, they must not be regarded as a complete cure for faulty intonation or sufficient in themselves to guarantee playing in tune. That is not only a question of technical training or musical knowledge although the habit of organized instrumental control and an understanding of the harmonic outline can be considered essential to it.

[1] From *Cello Playing of Today* by Maurice Eisenberg.

In the final analysis intonation comes from within. It is governed above all by the player's own critical desire and the keenness with which the exacting ear demands the placing of each note. Nothing can be taken for granted. The performer's attention must never be allowed to relax for an instant. It is all too easy for the ear to grow lazy without the instrumentalist being aware of it. Unless one remains constantly alert, alive to every possible weakness, even the simplest passages tend to go slightly off pitch.

Visualizing a phrase is an excellent stimulus to the vitality and perception of the aural faculties. When practising a difficult work players should accustom themselves to seeing the notes in imagination as steps going up and down a ladder, not merely as markings on a stave. In performance this will contribute to that intensity of concentration which can force muscles to achieve the desired results.

DOUBLE EXTENSIONS

Of all Casals's innovations, probably the most far-reaching concerns the physical development of the left hand. He trained it to become so pliable that the fingers could stretch a perfect fourth, say from the first position B on the A string to the fourth finger E, without a jump or slide. At the time of his debut this idea was revolutionary. It was immediately recognized as an outstanding feature of his technique but it was only after the appearance of Diran Alexanien's book, *The Technique of the Violoncello*, more than twenty years later, that cellists in general realized they might learn to make use of it personally.

For the sake of inexperienced players let it be said at once that big extensions should only be attempted when the fingers are ready for them. The necessity of preparing the hand patiently and logically cannot be too strongly stressed. If these fingerings are to take their rightful place as a natural part of the cellistic equipment a practical knowledge of 'instrumental geography' will also be needed.

As the stopping on the cello is largest in the lowest positions, experiments should be begun in the third and fourth positions where the notes are nearer together than in the first and second. Using the A string as our example, hold the D firmly with the first finger. All the fingers should be rounded and the second, third, and fourth poised respectively over ,E♭ E♮, and F. Then, without stiffening, make an extension by moving the whole hand (other than the index finger) upwards towards the bridge until the F can be played with the second finger. After enunciating it, the D should be sounded again as an octave over the open string to make sure that the first finger is still in place: there is a recurrent tendency to let it slip off its note in the wake of the rest of the hand.

Exercises like the following are useful:

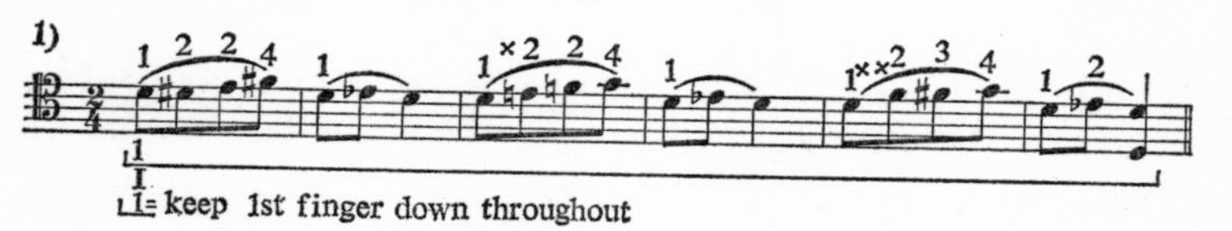

(later to be transposed down in steps of a semitone until the first finger reaches B in the first position), and:

(only to be worked in the positions for which it is written). These drills should be practised slowly at first and then a little quicker, but *never for too long at a time.*

The fingers should also be trained, by easy stages, to

stretch an octave between the first and fourth fingers on adjacent strings. Start by playing G on the A string, fourth finger in the fourth position. Holding this note firmly with the little finger, extend the first backwards over the D string until it is above the third position G. Both notes should then be played together as a semibreve (or whole-note). Immediately afterwards the hand should relax itself off the strings. It is good to repeat this a couple of times and then to practise something else before returning to it. When the hand can hold the Gs in comfort—and not before!—the octave F♯ should be worked, then octave F♮ and finally E. Never continue to hold the notes if the muscles become stiff or tired.

When practising extensions the hand and arm must remain basically relaxed so that the arm-weight and the intensity of the player can still pass freely on to the string through the fingers. As soon as the fingers have been stretched to their limit for a 'double extension' they should be closed up again. At first this will need a conscious effort, but eventually it should become an almost automatic reaction, resembling that of a rubber band released after having been held taut. The flexibility thus engendered will enable the whole hand to lend its weight to the finger vibrating the note after an extension. Furthermore, it will prevent the extension from impairing the tone: this is liable to occur if the fingers are kept outstretched for too long, either in anticipation, or on completion of the momentary effort involved.

The lower octaves of D♭ major scale, practised legato, provide a good vehicle in which to start applying the principles of double extensions to performance:

The first test comes when passing from B♭ on the C string to C on the G. This shift should be effected by stretching back the index finger in advance and not releasing the fourth until the C has been enunciated. The hand should close up immediately with the thumb opposite the coming D♭ and the second finger raised ready to fall on to it. The same procedure should be adopted in the subsequent changes of position. F♯ major scale:

which lends itself to similar treatment, presents greater difficulty because of the additional semitone to be covered by the change of string and position between A♯ on the C string and B on the G. Only an exceptionally large hand can stretch this and most players have to content themselves with extending the first finger back as far as the C♮ and letting the hand leap the remaining semitone at the last moment. There may be a temptation here to play the B with a straight finger. This could stiffen the hand. One should try to keep the joints slightly bent and avoid playing on the flat of the finger tip.

Big extensions were evolved with the dual purpose of giving additional facility to the finger work in moments of stress and eliminating certain slides and awkward finger placing which would interfere with the musical line. As such they are invaluable. It is often wise, however, to take simpler fingerings that are more restful for the hand. In general, extensions should only be employed where there is a logical reason for them.

TOUCH

The need for sensitivity in the finger tips does not apply solely to left-hand technique. When transmitting the human side of interpretation to their instruments string players are equally dependent on the reflexes in the fingers of the right hand. These latter are responsible for that sense of touch which can make or mar a fine performance. Its importance is underlined by the fact that many of the world's great executants invest hundreds of pounds and thousands of dollars in the purchase of Tourte bows in an endeavour to find the perfect vehicle through which to express themselves.

The first step towards its development lies in training the fingers to coax the tone from the string. Experiment in legato scales practised one, two, three, and four notes to a bow. The length of the stroke should be determined by the *minimum* amount of bow required to preserve a concentrated tone without allowing it to become heavy or stagnant. The stroke must be so well controlled that the changes of bow and string are inaudible. (See pp. 7–8.) The bow changes should be effected by an adjustment of the cushions of the finger tips on the 'frog' aided by straightening the little finger as the bow is carried towards the nut. Simple exercises incorporating this action, covering slurred notes on all four strings:

should also be worked in three different parts of the bow: near the nut, in the middle and at the point.

Eventually the fingers should be able to help almost subconsciously in bringing out the musical significance of the phrasing. At the outset, however, students should constantly remind themselves that accentuation and emphasis made by the bow is effected by tightening the grip on the 'frog' and quickening and subsequently retarding the speed with which the stick is swept across the string. For example, on long accented notes like those in the introductory bars of the Valentini E major sonata:

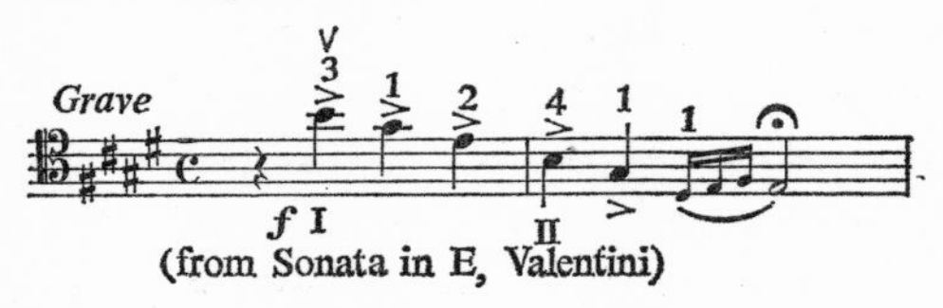

(from Sonata in E, Valentini)

the bow should move rapidly at the beginning of the stroke and gradually slow down. Meanwhile the player must listen critically to make sure that the brilliancy of the tone is preserved to the very end of each note.

Groups of quavers—four, six, and eight to a whole bow—played as if a *tenuto* line was printed over every note forms a good exercise for cultivating the habit of enunciating notes with the finger tips. Although at first sight this may seem like a slow-motion staccato, the two bowings have little in common. Staccato has its role as a mechanical effect. It is made up by alternately pushing and stopping the bow thus causing the hair to bite into the string and emit a rather harsh sound, 'tit-tit'. An entirely different inflexion is produced by slightly altering the speed of the bow *without stopping its movement* through the pressure of the fingers on the 'frog'. This creates a softer 'da-da', giving that reinforced, vocal expressiveness so important in phrases such as:

(from *Allegro Appassionato,* Saint-Saëns)

from Saint-Saëns' *Allegro Appassionato*.

The functions of the fingers on the bow are not confined

to controlling its actions when it is on the string. Its stroke frequently begins before and continues after the note is actually being played. Complete command of its actions when in the air between notes is essential if clumsiness is to be avoided. In rhythmic passages, for instance the main Rondo theme in the Finale of Beethoven's G minor sonata:

(from Finale of Sonata Op. 5. No.2, Beethoven)

and in the lighter sections of ancient solo sonatas there are numerous cases where mastery of the bow *off* the string is practically as important as the angle at which it strikes the notes. Such works should be practised phrase by phrase. Bow to and fro as if playing, but *instead of letting the hairs touch the strings keep them about an inch above them.* The percussion of the fingers of the vital left hand will provide sufficient sound.

The importance of controlling the bow action off the string, furthermore, is not only applicable when short strokes are indicated. A swing from above before playing a whole bow should often be employed to strengthen the attack on a sforzando or accent. There are innumerable examples of this in big, virile works like the Dvořák and Lalo concertos, Bloch's *Schelomo*, the first movement of the Beethoven D major sonata, and the Fugue in the Brahms E minor. We also find one in the first phrase of the Sammartini G major sonata:

(from Sonata in G, Sammartini)

which has to be played very rhythmically and with verve. The bow distribution must be planned to give the best results on the accents. Very little bow should be used on the up beat D in order to save as much as possible for the swing of the whole arm on the following quaver G. This note has a double significance, being both the tonic and the first beat of the bar. There is also, however, a second accent on the next note, the syncopated crotchet G, which requires élan. This needs an additional impetus best provided when the bow is already in motion before it comes down to strike the string. The sweep of the up bow should therefore be continued between the two Gs and its direction to down bow changed in the air. To accomplish this the fingers must remain in constant command of the stroke carrying the bow first beyond and then back to the string.

THUMB POSITION

Thumb position should become like second nature to the experienced cellist. To the uninitiated, however, it brings fresh problems and sometimes still engenders a sense of insecurity that can only be overcome by the confidence derived from serious study.

Luigi Boccherini was the first composer-cellist to realize the potentialities of the then unexplored upper ranges of the instrument, later known as the 'chanterelle'. Before his day C or C♯ in the seventh position on the A string were in general regarded as the highest notes in the cellistic compass although D and E were sometimes added by using a limited form of thumb position. Boccherini extended this to enable him to execute passages at the top of the fingerboard, thus providing a new instrumental dimension for his contemporaries and successors.

Some thumbs are much longer than others, so the exact position of the hand on the string in the thumb register varies according to the individual player. In all cases the top phalanx of the thumb has to be placed horizontally across two strings without touching a third. Gradually, through regular practice, little mounds will develop on the side of the thumb where it crosses the strings, one being close to the joint, the other near the nail. These correspond to the balls on the finger tips and should eventually enable the tone produced with the thumb to duplicate the quality produced by the fingers.

One important basic difference should be understood from the outset. In the lower positions the pulling backwards and downwards of the arm forms a 'clutch' which helps the fingers to sink into their notes backed by the accumulated weight of the arm and shoulder. In thumb position this asset is missing. To compensate for its absence the thumb has to act as a stopper on the string, pinning it to the fingerboard. The difficulty is to accomplish this without stiffening, and so paralysing the thumb. To combat this danger the elbow and shoulder should be very slightly raised thus allowing the weight to pass unhindered down the arm.

It often takes time to develop sufficient strength for the hand-weight to fall normally so that the thumb stops the strings automatically. Start by accustoming the thumb to find a natural home on the fifth:

ϙ = thumb

which is midway between the head of the cello and the

bridge. This fifth should be worked at intervals whilst practising until the thumb can find it as instinctively as the third finger can pitch either note separately. (See p. 22.) When so-doing the exact place of the arm in relation to the ribbing of the cello should be noted and memorized.

The next step is to train the third finger to find its way to the D on the A string to form an octave with the thumb D:

making certain that the weight is distributed equally between the notes. To accustom the hand to moving up and down the fingerboard while conserving this balance, work very short octave exercises on the lines of:

keeping the hand and lower arm in one piece. The shifts should be accomplished swiftly as if the whole hand were moving from one notch to another up a single movement. The first and second fingers should be used to support the third.

All students should familiarize themselves thoroughly with the placing of each tone and semitone within the initial octave. If this is done early in the study of thumb position it will form a model from which to work in different positions and on each pair of strings. Experiment first, therefore, in the third octave of both D major and D minor (melodic) scales fingered:

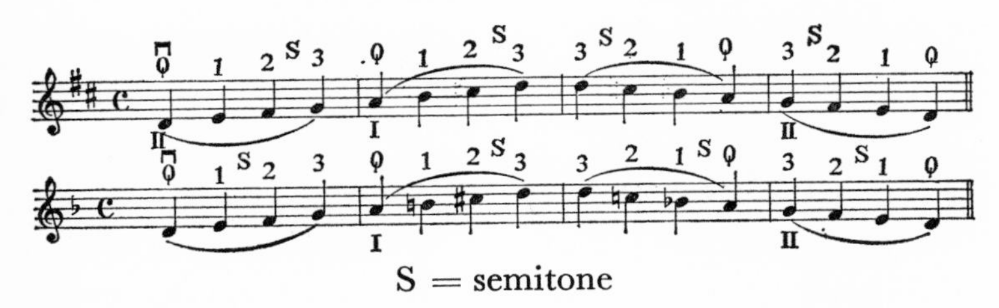

S = semitone

Use high, percussive finger articulation when ascending and pull back the fingers with a plucking movement when descending.

These scales should be followed by simple drills in the same position: these can be found in many specialized technique books. Work them with each finger rounded as far as possible and raised high before striking its note. Slow practice is recommended to begin with, to give the fingers time to reach the heart of their notes and allow the hand placings to be prepared in advance. Later, when a quicker speed is taken, every note must be clearly enunciated and strict attention paid to the purity of the tone and intonation.

Next, try short double-stopped passages in thirds and sixths. The shifts should be effected with the swift, concise movement already described. The adjustment of the fingers to the varying major and minor intervals naturally present complications. Advanced cellists should work sequences of mixed octaves and thirds, such as:

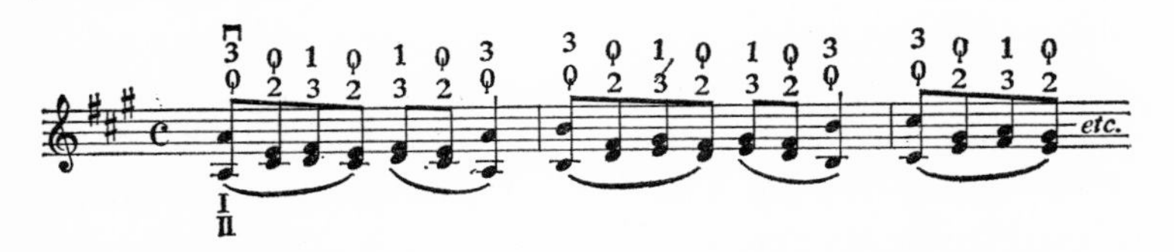

moulding the hand in advance so that the fingers are ready to fall on to all the notes in each bar when they leave the octave on the first beat.

Another useful drill is made up by working a scale up and down over two strings on the following lines:

continuing upwards until the thumb and third finger reach the tonic again. When the thumb reaches the leading note on the D string it is necessary to move it back a semitone to play the subdominant (D♮) on the A string without disturbing the fingers playing the intervening notes:[1]

This calls for a swift backwards movement of the thumb timed to take place at the precise moment that the third finger strikes the mediant, C♯.

BUDGETING PRACTICE TIME

Players often find themselves in trouble when first striving to steer a middle course in music making. They wish to play with spirit and their muscles become taut; they try not to stiffen and almost invariably lose intensity; they are determined to enunciate clearly and cleanly and discover so many interesting technical problems that they neglect the interpretation; or they get so immersed in the emotional aspect of the music that they become oblivious of blemishes in the style

[1] These drills and that marked on the preceding page will be found in a fuller and more advanced form in Chapter VI of Eisenberg's *Cello Playing of Today*.

and intonation. It is extremely hard for cellists whose instrument, owing to its size, requires a particularly well-adjusted balance between strength and relaxation to achieve a successful blending of heart, mind, and muscle, and guidance is frequently needed before a practical plan of study can be evolved.

All students wishing to make progress should work regularly at technique. This does not mean merely repeating formulas as a routine. It should also include listening to the sound produced in order to make sure that the exercises are being practised in a way that fulfils the complete purpose for which they were designed.

The percentage of practising time to be devoted to 'pure technique' depends largely on the individual pupil and the stage of his or her development. Ten to fifteen minutes in every hour might be taken as a rough estimate. More advanced players, however, generally find that after establishing the flexibility of the fingers and the equilibrium of the bow by a short 'run through' on scales and arpeggios, their most useful exercises are those they invent for themselves, founded in passages in concertos, sonatas and solos.

After such technical preliminaries cellists—especially those whose practising hours are limited—should turn at once to any new work they are learning. If tackling it alone, without the help of a teacher, it is good to begin by studying the *piano* score. While so-doing, hum or sing the cello part and try to get an idea of the shape and character of the composition. Make a point of memorizing the sound of the harmonic progressions: hearing them in imagination will be of the greatest assistance in building up a musicianly picture of the work. Then take the cello and start practising it phrase by phrase.

The average person, if at all musical, phrases more or less intuitively when singing. On an instrument, however, the diverse complexities of the technique often cause players to perform a passage contrary to how they would sing it. Consequently the following steps are recommended. Hum the melody before attempting to play it on the cello. Next, sing it again *simultaneously articulating the notes on the instrument with the left hand.* Immediately afterwards, repeat it a third time and while singing and fingering it in the same way *also mime the strokes of the bow,* carrying the stick over the strings without touching them. (See p. 29.) Both hands will thus grow accustomed to demanding the right movements to convey the shape of the phrase as the cellist feels it. This will be appreciated when taking it a fourth time, played as written.

Meanwhile the fingerings and bowings should have been chosen. No definite rules can be given here as each hand is different and every composition presents its own problems. This personal factor should be taken into account when considering the markings suggested in transcriptions, which are not necessarily the best for everyone. In making a decision, the main guide-lines should be: (1) the lie of the passage, (2) which finger placings are the most comfortable and conducive to fine intonation, and (3) the speed, lilt, inflexion and punctuation of the passages in question.

Good punctuation is as important in music as correct breathing in elocution. Not only is it essential to the vitality of a performance, it also provides an infinitesimal resting place where the intensity in the arms and fingers can be momentarily relaxed without detriment to the continuity of the tone. On this account cellists who have mastered the art of musical punctuation will have solved one of the major problems jointly affecting technique and interpretation.

First try to discover which notes require emphasis and which constitute the equivalent of a comma or semicolon. On the latter, slow down the vibrato and lighten the bow almost imperceptibly, sometimes practically stopping it. This should create a tiny respite which will allow the music and the player to breathe.

In developing this idea, work a few bars very slowly, the hand movements resembling those in a slow-motion film. Never lose sight of the real nature of the music, that is to say when an Allegro is worked Adagio the style should be the same as when it is subsequently played up to time. Ultimately the reactions should become almost subconscious, as if when certain notes were reached they said 'relax' to the muscles concerned. The Allegro from Schumann's 'Adagio and Allegro' (Op. 70) provides an illustration of this:

(from *Adagio and Allegro*. Op. 70, Schumann)

After having taken a work apart, practising the extensions, jumps, shifts and slides from note to note and making up little exercises to develop the various tactile reflexes, the details should be fitted together into a general framework. Before ending the daily session at the instrument, try out the results by playing the piece or movement through without stopping. Take it slowly at first so that the details can be planned in advance, but aim at performing it a little nearer the correct speed and with increasing freedom and certainty each day. Working thus, the student gradually becomes identified with the music and starts interpreting it with conviction and insight while preserving respect for the indications of the score. This system, applied to easy solos, enables even relatively elementary players to give a musical and well balanced performance.

PART TWO

Tone Production in the Higher Registers

THE ROLE OF THE INDEX FINGER

A TROUBLED cellist once wrote: 'My big trial is playing in the higher and thumb positions. The first finger seems cramped while using the thumb and does not lie on the string correctly, as the nail cuts the string. I find it difficult to get a good tone both with and without the thumb on the fingerboard. Perhaps there is some method you could recommend ?

The answ'er to his direct question is 'Yes'. There are many excellent manuals that can be suggested according to the proficiency of the player, Cossmann, Grützmacher, Popper, Servais, to mention just a few. Some are studies rather than 'methods' but all are invaluable providing that they are applied in the right way. It is upon this matter of application—which should be individual—that everything depends.

Even exercises must be worked with the idea of making them sound pleasant and musical. Otherwise they will defeat their purpose: to develop greater technical command for use in interpreting the music.

It is generally assumed that less advanced cellists find it easier to do this in the lower positions. In the lowest register, which consists of the first four positions, the thumb should be opposite the second finger. Although it is kept behind the neck of the cello and the fingers are over the strings, it moves with the hand from one position to another. In the second register, made up of the fifth, sixth, and seventh positions, the thumb remains in the crook of the neck while the hand travels up the fingerboard on its own. In the third, usually known as thumb position, the thumb is placed *on* the strings so that it can be shifted with the hand and used when necessary to play notes. As the position of the thumb is responsible, to a large extent, for the main difference in the hand placing in the various registers, it seems obvious that any trouble encountered will probably be due to faulty placing of the fingers in relation to the thumb, a question which becomes more complex in the higher registers.

When learning to master new difficulties or to correct weaknesses it is always good to work from a familiar base. Analyse the actions employed there, compare them to what will be required elsewhere and try to adapt them to meet fresh conditions. If players produce their best tone in the first position, take it as a 'key' to which to revert repeatedly in order to assess how far the same technique can be applied farther up the cello.

The placing of the index finger is vitally important to that of the other three. Start, therefore, by placing a series of sustained, vibrated Bs in the first position on the A string. The tone should be as full as possible without forcing. When it sounds satisfactory, stop bowing but continue vibrating, studying the actions of the left hand, fingers, and arm. Note and memorize their positions. It should be found that the hand is compactly placed with the second, third, and fourth fingers grouped together over the first. The latter should be pointing slightly in the direction of the bridge, its tip, vibrating the string, turned a little towards its outer side. As the forearm must be in one piece from the elbow to the finger tip in order that the arm weight can flow naturally through the hand on to the string, the upper arm should never be allowed to hang down.

Adopting this hand position, begin working exercises for moving about the A string with the index finger. First take:

and follow it with:

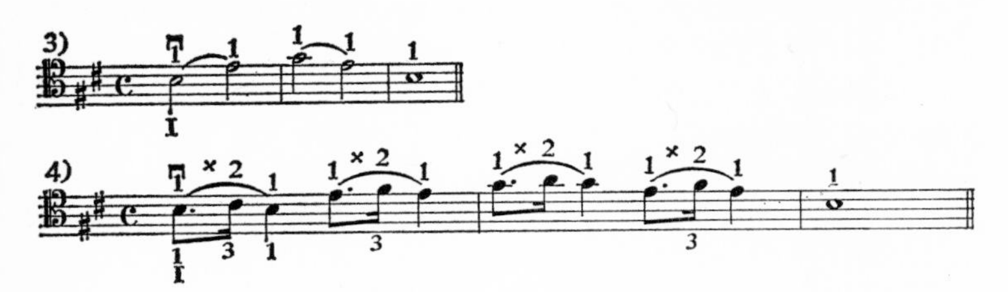

and:

making sure that the tone quality does not alter. Check up specifically on the similarities and differences in the hand placings in the various positions. In the fourth, the index finger should be rather more on its side than in the first. Moreover, as the elbow should be level with the hand throughout the lower register, once the thumb reaches the crook of the neck the upper arm need no longer be almost horizontal as in the first position. In the sixth and seventh the first finger is turned further away from the thumb and becomes more elongated: this should not disturb the tone if the top joint remains slightly curved and the fingers do not become stiff. As long as the hand is flexible and the fingers help each other it should be possible to acquire as much tonal freedom in this register as in the lower one.

When the placings of the first finger are established, work exercises up and down the strings chromatically, on the lines of:

At the outset, practise it slowly, without any vibrato. Afterwards also treat it as a drill for finger articulation, playing it at a fairly rapid pace. In both instances keep the first finger on the string throughout. Finally, work it with vibrato at a moderate pace, letting go with the first finger immediately the third finger enunciates its note so that each finger will learn to add its weight to the others.

Jumps of an octave on the same string should be practised next:

Here players will find that if the tone is to retain its clarity in both registers it will be necessary to compensate for the shortening of the vibrating string caused by the hand moving up the fingerboard. This involves 'focusing' the tone, i.e. using greater velocity in the bowing and stroking the strings nearer the bridge on the higher notes as well as increasing the intensity of the vibrato. These drills provide an excellent means through which to start working at this important aspect of technique.

THE ROLE OF THE THUMB

The specific, as opposed to the general, cause of awkward

finger placing in thumb position can usually be traced to a failure in raising the knuckles sufficiently high above the strings to enable the notes to be articulated from the same height as in the lower registers.

In thumb position the thumb and the finger tips are on the same level whereas elsewhere they are separated by both the neck of the cello and the fingerboard. Consequently in the thumb registers the back of the hand no longer has a natural prop which automatically lifts it to its requisite position. Furthermore, when first striving to pin two strings to the wood with the top phalanx of the thumb, the effort involved in obtaining the necessary strength is apt to lead to exaggerations. As a result, instead of only pushing down from the elbow to the thumb, many make the mistake of simultaneously pressing inwards with the hand. This brings the knuckles so close to the string that it is impossible for the fingers to enunciate their notes either at the correct angle or with enough vitality to produce a ringing tone.

The problem lies in combining the firmness needed in the thumb with the flexibility essential to the fingers without letting either interfere with the other. A simple experiment should show students whether the hand and knuckles are rightly placed. Start by playing:

then, without stopping, shift the hand up the D string to play the same notes an octave higher with the same fingering. DO NOT AS YET PUT THE THUMB ON THE STRINGS: instead, place it *under the fingerboard*, approximately opposite the first finger. This latter should be rounded and turned very slightly on its side while the hand points almost imperceptibly towards the bridge. Listen to the tone and compare it to that produced in the first position and make careful note of the placing of the whole hand unit. Leaving this undisturbed lift the thumb on to the D and A strings to stop the D–A fifth, and play:

preserving the same quality and quantity of tone and trying to prevent the knuckles and finger joints from caving in.

Unless this can be satisfactorily accomplished, exercises should be worked to strengthen the hand. Clamp down the thumb over the upper strings on the D–A fifth with the fingers tightly rolled *inside* the palm of the hand. This will force the knuckles upward while the level of the wrist remains unchanged, thus permitting the arm weight to pass freely into the thumb.

Maintaining this position of the hand and fingers next work short passages in fifths, such as:

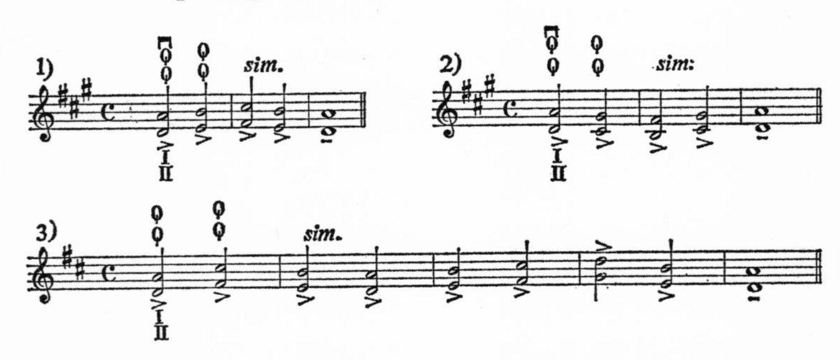

avoiding the diminished interval on the leading note. Physically this should reinforce the feeling that the thumb is an integral part of the forearm unit and accustom it to moving as directed by the elbow joint. It will also underline the necessity of lifting the elbow sufficiently to prevent the lower arm from coming into contact with the side of the cello when changing position. In addition, used towards the top of the fingerboard:

it should reveal how the hand, on approaching the bridge, is influenced by the angle of the arm, pulling automatically and infinitesimally away from the thumb which must remain horizontal, across the strings. Ultimately this will affect the finger placings in the highest part of the instrumental register.

Double-stopped drills in which a perfect fifth alternates with a variety of intervals should be practised next. Begin as before on the D–A fifth which should again be stopped by the thumb while the fingers are curled into the palm of the hand. Without disturbing the angle of the knuckles release the fingers, drawing them up until they stand high above the strings, held together like a broad hook, with the top joints rounded. Then bring them down so that the first finger strikes its note supported by the weight of all the rest:

To avoid touching the nail, the finger should be turned a trifle more to one side on the A string on which, at the outset, fingered notes are usually found to lie less naturally than on the D. When its placing can be assured on both strings, amplify this exercise to include intervals played by the second and third fingers, like:

enunciating the notes in a similar way. Afterwards experiment with other note patterns, applying the drills, as experience is gained, to all parts of the thumb register.

With some hands it is advisable to continue strengthening the muscles for some time by returning the fingers to their temporary home inside the palm upon reaching the final fifth when practising these exercises. The habit should be discarded, however, as soon as possible. When dispensing with it, players might find it helpful to realize that the hand should retain an oval shape, as if an egg were being held between the string and the inner juncture of the knuckles and the fingers.

THE IMPORTANCE OF DOUBLE STOPPING

Unfortunately, the tendency of the knuckles to cave in when playing in thumb position is apt to be recurrent, especially when students can only spend a relatively short time each day at the cello. It is therefore wise to adopt measures to ensure against a relapse. One of the most successful is to practise scales in double stopping using a uniform fingering which includes a thumb note throughout. Take for example those in:

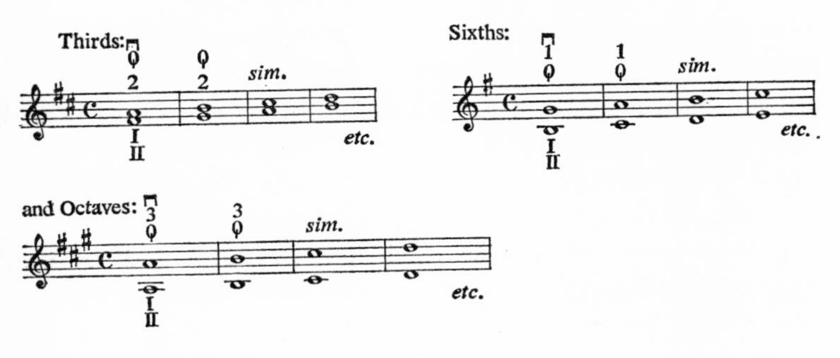

Scales in fourths:

although most valuable, are frequently neglected, probably because they sound so ugly! They literally force the hands to form a semi-circular arc from the wrist to the finger tip over the base of the horizontal thumb.

In general the difficulty lies in distributing the weight evenly on both strings. When shifting the whole hand unit in double-stopped passages the thumb normally bears the main weight although when using the first finger it should share this responsibility. Many players concentrate too exclusively on the higher note, regardless of whether it is played by the thumb or a finger. This error, by disturbing the balance of the whole hand, can adversely affect the tone and must be consciously avoided.

Once the thumb has been placed across the strings it should not be taken off them except: (1) to return to its place behind the neck, (2) to play a note on a string which is not already covered by its fifth, (3) when it is necessary to perform a harmonic, or (4) at the close of the passage, movement or piece concerned. Both the thumb and the fingers, however, have to be taught to move up and down the string independently, as this is often necessary in performance. Furthermore, advanced cellists find that the hand is freer, both when vibrating lyrical phrases and when executing rapid passage work, if it is not 'crowded' by the thumb remaining constantly a tone or a semitone behind the index finger, especially in the upper ranges of the instrumental compass.

Here are a few exercises for developing facility in this aspect of technique:[1]

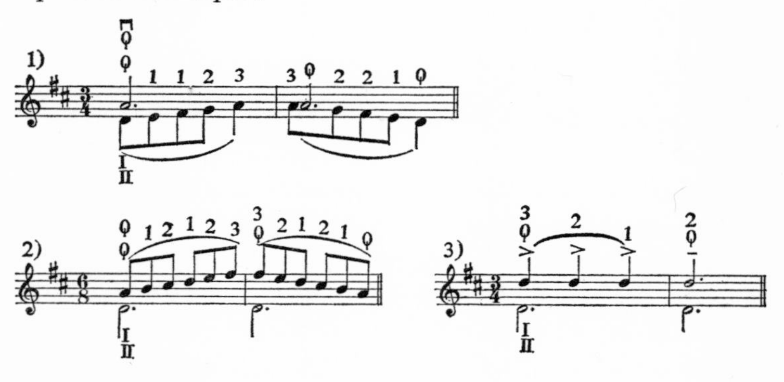

Afterwards take:

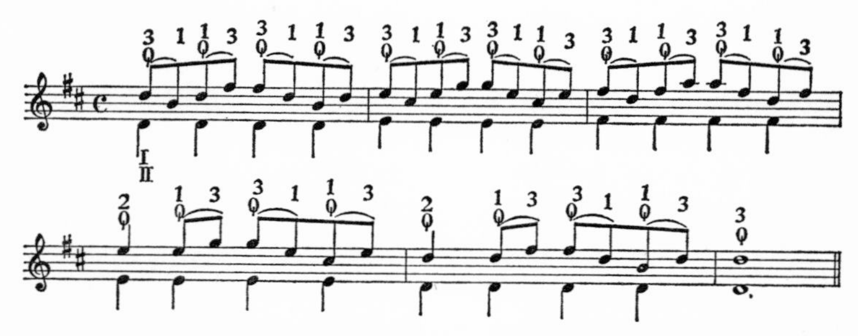

[1] Other exercises on these lines will be found in *Cello Playing of Today* by Maurice Eisenberg.

in which the fingers move as a block, away from the stationary thumb and the space varies between the stopped fifth and the elongated first finger. Follow this by others:

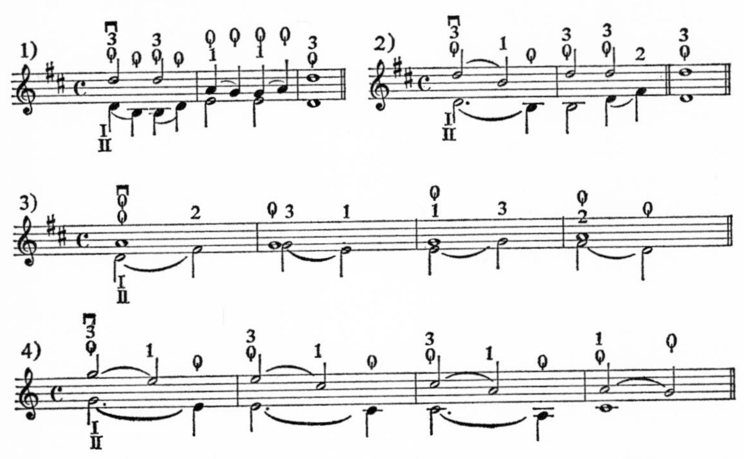

where the thumb, still at right angles to the strings, acts on its own. These ideas should likewise be applied later in the higher octaves of all diatonic three and four octave scales.

The little finger is rarely used in the thumb registers because of its restricted length. Nevertheless, it is sometimes needed, so one dare not neglect it. The drills in the thumb section of Cossman's *Cello Studies* can be recommended to develop its percussive powers but when working at them, students should be careful never to drag the knuckles down in an effort to strengthen its articulation. Like the other three, it should be pointed towards the bridge whenever possible.

The thumb also has to be trained to play isolated notes in the lower register to simplify certain fingerings. This means that it has to leave and return to its position behind the neck to play a stopped note on the string without disturbing the hand placing while the fingers continue to sing their notes. Drills should be worked on the lines of:

the last being designed as a pattern for others useful when preparing the hand to shift smoothly into normal thumb position from lower down the fingerboard.

So far only the purely technical side of our correspondent's problems have been discussed. For complete success, muscular effort must be directed by a definite desire for musical quality. In order to produce beautiful sounds it is necessary to hear in imagination the colour, texture, and nuance that is desired.

Many inexperienced cellists seem to be constrained in thumb position. They instinctively fight shy of vibrating with the thumb. Perhaps they fear it will upset the intonation, or it may simply be that the hand and arm feel constricted when the thumb is no longer giving support behind the neck of the cello.

These inhibitions must be mastered. The whole forearm unit from the elbow to the finger tips *including the thumb* should be vibrant, whether the thumb is playing a note or merely holding down the strings. The drills in fifths, described on pages 46 and 47, can be adapted to these ends. Also add others, like:

Concentrate the weight of the fingers behind whichever digit is vibrating and try to vibrate each exercise as a phrase, without stopping the oscillations. In addition, without interfering with this, practise enunciating and stressing individual notes through a quickening or a renewal of the vibrations. Finally, remember that if the bow crosses the string at a wrong angle, too far or too near the bridge, or if it is too heavy or slow-moving, it can discount the best work of the left hand.

PART THREE

Cello Playing for the Adult Beginner

GENERAL PROBLEMS

ADULT BEGINNERS on the cello are usually faced with certain specific problems. In some ways they have an advantage over younger pupils, being more mature and thus better equipped to understand the reasons behind the instruction they are given. On the other hand, from a purely physical standpoint they are often slightly handicapped because their fingers are no longer as flexible as in childhood and the muscles tend to resist unaccustomed demands.

In assessing the qualities that are vital to them, will-power must be given high priority. Naturally, a basic love of music in general and sympathy with the fundamental characteristics of their chosen instrument in particular are always essential: it is to be assumed that all who start learning have these, at least to some extent. In themselves, however, they are not enough, any more than, at the highest level, fleetness of finger without musical vision constitutes true artistry. Prospective players need to bring something more to their endeavours and many will discover that dogged determination is required before the initial obstacles can be surmounted and they become free to derive joy from their music making.

Nowadays so much is done to stimulate the young that the standard of cello playing among students is higher than at any time in history. An increasing number of children are learning and from these groups players not infrequently emerge with talent far above the average. They are fortunate in their generation and there is always room at the top.

This situation, wholly admirable as it is, tends to be rather inhibiting to older students. They may have wished to learn in their school days and feel frustrated because they had no opportunity to do so. Even today one finds grown-up late-starters without any prior theoretical knowledge, who had to master the intricacies of time values, keys, and clefs on their own from reading up the subjects in books. Yet some take this for granted and consider the ability to play simple pieces for pleasure with beauty of tone, purity of intonation and perfect rhythm to be their logical and legitimate objective.

So many details are inherent to the development of sufficient technique to enable them to achieve this aim that it is hardly surprising if some students become rather despondent in the earlier stages. Many find it hard to stretch the fingers from note to note in the first and half positions, especially when extensions are involved: others have trouble in ascertaining whether they are playing quite in tune. Cellists in either category should supplement drills on a single string by working finger-patterns over a harmonic background provided by the drone of a 'pedal note' played on an adjacent open string. Take:

which can also be adapted to the two upper strings. Played a bar to a whole bow these exercises will likewise help to train the right arm to move in and out naturally so that while preserving a unified arm action the individual joints—i.e. the elbow, wrist, and knuckles—flex themselves automatically. (See p. 6.)

Later, try an exercise like:

designed to accustom the index finger to moving smoothly between its different placements in the half and first positions when the latter is 'extended backwards'. As the hand stretches out in bar 2 and contracts just before bar 4, the first finger is straightened and subsequently rounded again, its *tip* remaining on the B♭. Meanwhile the thumb should be shifted along the neck of the cello so that it is always opposite the second finger. Only the first finger should be subject to a change of direction, the rest of the unit keeps its original shape.

Practically all sensitive cellists, irrespective of status, eventually experience a desire to vibrate the fingers in order to bring out the expressive content of the music. This can also present a problem to those who start learning rather late in life. Unless the muscles are pliable, it is difficult, at the outset, to keep the hand relaxed without being so loose that the finger tip slips about the string. The action of the whole hand here might be likened to that of the extending first finger insomuch as both have to be taught to contract and stretch out again while performing a note *without letting this disturb the texture and continuity of the tone*. It is a question of utilizing the weight of all the fingers grouped over the one vibrating its note and, while still playing it, of moving them away from it preparatory to enunciating the coming note on which the fingers should all close up again.

Many adult beginners have a gift for the instrument which they use with great intelligence. Those who derive most from their work, however, are the brave ones who never give in. Their will-power is such that, to paraphrase

Kipling, it forces 'heart and nerve and sinew to serve their turn . . . and so hold on'.

COMBINING FIRMNESS WITH FLEXIBILITY

Adult beginners often find it particularly difficult to avoid stiffness when first training the fingers to act with strength and precision. The nervous tension engendered by striving to manipulate bones and muscles in unfamiliar ways is apt to create temporary rigidity. Yet unless the hands acquire a basic firmness it will be impossible for them to hold down the strings and produce real tone. Moreover, to achieve clarity of diction on the cello the fingers must be capable of clear, percussive articulation. The student's first objective should therefore be to use the natural arm weight as a background from which to build a strong, flexible technique.

Inexperienced cellists often have trouble in keeping the fingers in place on their notes in first position passages where all the fingers are employed. It takes time before the hand is sufficiently supple to stretch out to play four widely spaced semitones in this register without a sustained effort of concentration. Take, for example, the following note-pattern:

and play it twice through without stopping. It will probably be found that when the final E is reached the first finger will have slipped almost as far up the string as the F.

In this register the stopping is so big that in most cases the fingers require very special training before they can cover the distances involved in comfort. Many aspiring players have to remain on their guard for some time to prevent the hand from automatically closing up and bringing the fingers too near each other. The long-accepted device of testing the intonation by 'getting an octave' from an open string to the little finger:

in the first position before starting to play cannot be considered wholly satisfactory because it offers no proof that any finger other than the fourth is in tune. It is better to treat the index finger, which in this position is a whole tone above the open string, as the primary gauge. Once its place has been established one can build upwards to the fourth finger, and on reaching it try it as an octave, as an additional check before returning to the first finger:

Before starting to play make sure that the thumb is on the neck of the cello opposite the home of the second finger and that the elbow is approximately level with the hand. Next practise:

working it very slowly until the fingered note can be pitched with comparative certainty. Sink into it from above with a rounded finger which, as it descends, has the full support of the other fingers grouped over it. The knuckles and the back of the hand should be raised well above the fingerboard and the curved fingers held still higher, like a broad hook, before coming down to strike the note. A most helpful initial exercise for encouraging relaxation consists of lifting the hand imperceptibly while the tip of the index finger pins the string firmly to the wood.

Contact with the string should be made towards the outer side of the cushion of the first finger rather than straight across its tip. This habit, once established, will accustom the player to a placing that will later prove invaluable when making extensions or shifting to higher positions. The hand is always most comfortable when the fingers can point slightly downwards towards the bridge. (See p. 12.)

The importance of developing a strong grip with the first finger cannot be over-emphasized. Directly its placing is 'set' more drills should be added. The following should be worked on all the strings:

memorizing the feeling of the finger spacing from note to note.

As the little finger is shorter than the others, when it is used after the third the latter should be rather straighter than usual and turned very slightly towards the place that the fourth finger is to occupy. In a lesser degree the second finger can act in a similar way, *providing that it is not sounding a note which is a whole tone behind the fourth* (as it does in bar 6 of the above). In such cases, a conscious stretch between the fingers will probably be needed.

Short exercises, like slow-motion preparatory trill studies can be advocated. Try:

repeating each bar several times. A swift but slight downward movement of the whole forearm from the elbow to the wrist should be used to reinforce the finger articulation. The whole unit, however, should raise itself immediately afterwards while the lower finger continues to sing the basic note. This drill should be practised on all the strings in turn.

At this elementary stage as many fingers as possible should be kept on the string. For example, the first should remain in its place when the second holds its note and both the first and the second while the third is playing (bar 4). When the third strikes a note above the first (bar 2), the second finger should fall on to the string with the third, and so on. In general the third and fourth fingers are weaker than the first and second, so it will probably take longer before they become strong and flexible. Left-hand percussion drills (see pp. 9–10) will be useful in this connection.

SIMPLE EXTENSIONS

If a Gallup poll were taken with the purpose of discovering what was the most troublesome single problem encountered by the adult beginner on the cello, in all probability the word 'extensions' would head the list by a clear majority. Even with children, hands are often resistant at first to a sideways stretch between the fingers. This tendency is still more pronounced with grown-ups whose muscles, in general, are less pliable.

The left hand can be prepared, to a considerable extent, by preliminary work away from the instrument. Start by massaging it with the fingers of the right hand, gently twisting each digit in its socket in turn while the unit as a whole remains relaxed and undisturbed by these manipulations. Next, place the fingers of the right hand (first using two together and later three) between each pair in the left hand: this should increase their spacing without forcing the muscles. After this hold the left hand upwards and make a V sign between the first and second fingers.

Follow these measures by placing the left hand on a table with the fingers rounded and the knuckles raised. Arrange it so that the thumb is on its inner side, opposite the second finger, thus duplicating their respective positions above and under the neck of the cello. Holding this placing, move the index finger sideways, to and fro, away from and back towards the second finger.

This should help to free the muscles. However, the real test comes when transferring these actions to the instrument. There are two different kinds of whole-tone extensions between the first and second fingers which are in constant use. One occurs when stretching upwards to play, say:

and the other when extending backwards to a lower note in a passage such as:

Most students find that the first type is the more difficult. It can be practised, to begin with, in the lowest octave of A minor scale melodic form, ascending.

Directly the rounded index finger is firmly in place on the E (bar III) start moving the hand away from it. Make certain that the thumb shifts up the neck of the cello towards the bridge together with the extending second finger. When so doing also be careful that the thumb does not press unduly against the wood, stiffening the hand: it should move loosely up and down the neck without strain.

Pulling the hand away from the first finger should automatically cause the latter to become elongated, that is to say less curved. This will provide a wider space between its tip and that of the second finger which should thus be brought into position to fall on to the F♯. Opening out the hand will likewise bring the third and fourth fingers into 'squared' placing (see p. 12) and so enable the little finger in its turn to drop on to the G♯.

When the E–F♯–G♯ have been played in tune and the open string A has been reached, take the hand off the cello and relax the fingers. At the outset, however, just before doing this, play the first finger E again, either with the open string A or immediately after it, to make sure that the index finger has not slipped off its note.

The stability of the first finger in an upward extension can also be tested by working:

in which the open string D provides a stable measure of comparison for the intonation when closing up the hand after an extension. In this note pattern the change of hand placing should occur while playing the second E.

Extensions should be practised on all strings until they can be made almost subconsciously. Here are two suggestions to serve as models:

from which players can evolve their own experimental drills. In working them the elbow should always be kept in a line with the hand. If it is allowed to hang down it will pull the fingers off their notes.

Backward extensions, for example from G to B♭, can be worked in G minor scale melodic form, descending:

The index finger should act independently while the rest of the hand unit, including the thumb, remains stationary. The first finger should straighten itself as it moves along the string towards the head of the cello, to which it should point. As soon as there is no further reason for it to be outstretched it should, however, be brought back to normal first position placing, a semitone behind the second finger. In the scale quoted above this change-over can take place while playing the open string D. Where no such opportunities exist, it should be shifted up the string inaudibly during the performance of a note stopped by one of the other fingers.

Further facility in this backward extension finger movement can be gained by practising short drills on one string like:

FREEDOM OF THE WRIST

As regards bowing, the greatest difficulty for most adult beginners probably consists of acquiring freedom of movement in the wrist. At early lessons it is relatively easy to understand that the wrist should be high at the nut and lower at the point. Many elementary cellists, however, run into trouble when first attempting to put these precepts into practice in consecutive whole bow drills that have to be played without a break of tone. In the initial stages, sometimes the more the pupil tries, the harder it seems, because undue effort frequently leads to increased nervous tension.

Actually, the wrist is rarely solely responsible for such defects. Although each section of the arm and every joint in it must at times be treated individually, fundamentally they form part of a single entity. As such they are physically influenced by each other. For instance, after playing an up bow it is almost impossible to bring the wrist back to its proper down bow position at the nut unless the elbow and upper arm also return to their original 'nut' placings. In addition, the fingers, particularly the first and fourth, have to straighten themselves after being rounded for playing at the point.

A sense of cohesion can usually be developed by training the whole arm to move in and out naturally, without sounding the strings, through the expedient already recommended in these pages (see p. 7) of shifting the hand backwards and forwards along the bow stick. This drill can be amplified in several ways that should help to make the wrist movement more automatic. The object is to combine control of the arm on a long stroke with facility in using it sectionally to play shorter notes.

Start as before with both hands together at the point, wrists high, and the bow held firmly in place with the *left* hand, and move the right hand along the bow to the frog. Unless the student has an exceptionally long arm, it will be found that in order to reach this extremity of the bow the wrist will have to lower itself, the back of the hand become flatter and the fingers more rounded. Keeping this new position intact, grip the nut and begin pushing the bow inwards on an up stroke:

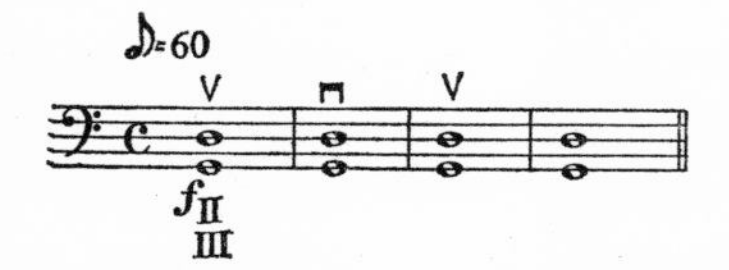

While playing the up bow the fingers, hand, wrist and arm should gradually regain their regular 'nut' position and be ready for the coming down bow. As soon as the right hand takes command, the left should release its hold on the point, remaining in place, just above the stick without touching the wood, the fingers in front of it and the thumb behind. The bow can then pass under the hand unit as if it were a short tunnel.

This is an excellent way to check up on the angle of the stroke. If it is not under control, moving parallel to the bridge, the bow will touch one of the sides of the 'tunnel', automatically reminding the cellist to straighten it by adapting the finger pressure on the frog. After the G–D fifth has been worked, the drill should be applied on the other pairs of open strings.

A further variation can be evolved by drawing out the right arm in the same way, but when the hand reaches the frog, instead of immediately pushing in on a slow up bow, play:

only using as much bow on the shorter notes as can be supplied by the wrist and finger action. At first the distances covered may be very short but with practice it should soon become longer.

Next, hold the bow on the string at the *centre* with the *left* hand and place the right arm over the nut just above the wrist. (In this exercise the thumb should not be separated from the fingers by the stick.) Keeping the hand and fingers suspended as loosely and freely as possible, work different kinds of wrist movements for a few moments without playing: (1) lift the hand unit up and down, (2) swing it from side to side, and (3) describe a circle with it. When these actions can be accomplished without any feeling of strain, work them holding a pencil placed between the second finger and the thumb, arranging the other fingers as if they were on the nut of a bow. This will help to solve that dual problem of simultaneously gripping the frog with the digits and maintaining flexibility in the wrist.

The bowing exercises suggested on pages 6 and 7, should be incorporated early in studentship. In addition, players should make use of over-string bow drills to train the wrist and fingers directly they can control the stroke on single notes. Begin with:

counting a slow eight in each bar. Follow this with exercises that involve playing each string alternately:

repeating each group several times without stopping. Continuity of tone should be preserved throughout. Try to keep the arm on the same level on both strings and to effect the changes of string by means of the finger and wrist movement. The fingers should be straighter on the lower string than on the higher one, no matter in which direction the bow is travelling. Afterwards apply these exercises to the other strings and also begin them on the higher notes.

TRILLS

Trill practice should be introduced as soon as the first and second fingers can pin their notes firmly to the fingerboard in the first position. Adult beginners are apt, mistakenly, to regard this aspect of cello playing as beyond their present scope. Yet trills and other ornaments are frequently found in the arrangements of ancient airs and dances which constitute the greater part of their working literature in the early stages of studentship. It is really a matter of necessity for them to try to cultivate a trill.

Furthermore, practising trills develops a combination of speed, strength and agility in the fingers which will benefit left-hand technique as a whole. The inclusion of ornamentation in so-called simple solos was surely not entirely due to chance. Most of them were transcribed by eminent teachers who must have known how helpful it would be if elementary cellists were encouraged to assimilate the flexibility thus gained in a natural way.

The trill is not confined to the music of any one era. Much of the other ornamentation in vogue during the seventeenth and eighteenth centuries has become obsolete. The trill, however, remains as does the appoggiatura:

the mordent:

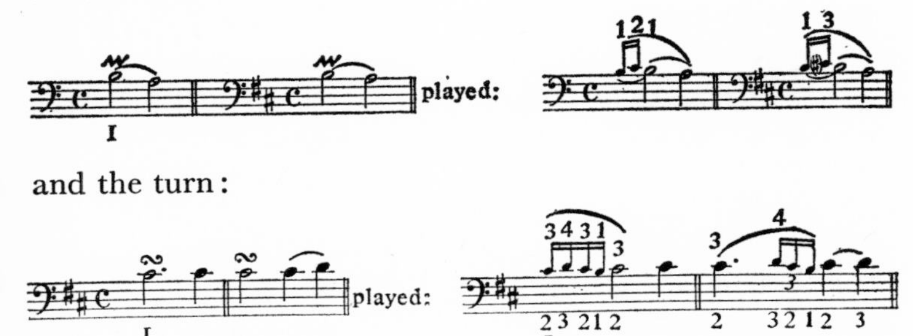

and the turn:

Although the trill is used the most often and is subject to innumerable changes of style and pace, it is actually the third step in present-day ornamentation. First comes the appoggiatura with its single auxiliary note and then the mordant with its 'shake' of two notes. It is in this order that they should be studied on the cello.

In working them, they can often be combined with other drills. Take, for instance, sustained notes played with the index finger in the first position:

which is recommended to establish the balance of weight between the arms and a controlled movement of the right arm, and practise it:

on all the strings in turn. Leave the C to the last as, being the thickest and the farthest for the fingers to stretch, it is the most difficult of the four to handle. Be sure the index finger is firmly in place throughout. While it is playing its note, prepare the other fingers to descend swiftly on to the appoggiatura by holding them high above the string, grouped together with the tips rounded. Directly the grace note has been articulated draw them up again with equal rapidity. Later, increase the number of notes in the ornament,

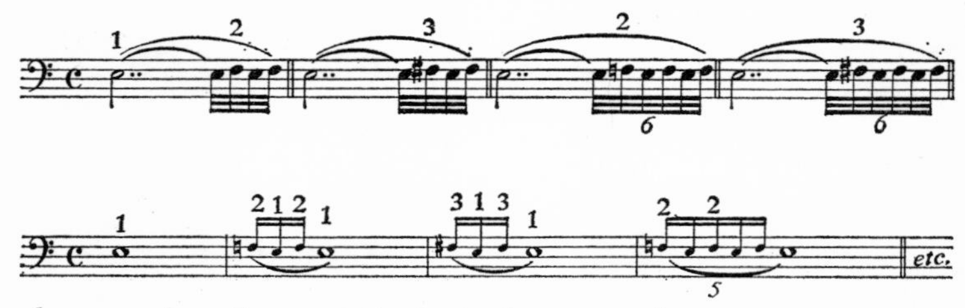

always using the same technical approach.

Mordents (or shakes) can be incorporated in the Eisenberg 'warming up' exercises covering all four strings:[1]

The position of the fingers before and after the string is struck is the same as in the appoggiatura. The swifter the percussive movement, the better the results will be. Begin by keeping to the first six bars, then gradually add those requiring 2–3, 2–4, and 3–4 fingering. Subsequently try a double mordent (two shakes), and then three or four shakes, which leads up to a short trill.

Trills rarely consist of a series of absolutely equal notes: instead they generally get faster as they proceed. Consequently it is often impractical to raise the fingers as high after each shake on a trill as after a single shake on a mordent. They start alike, but as the speed increases there will not be time to draw up the fingers to their full height. This is particularly noticeable in long trills such as are found in a Sarabande, and those in quicker dances like a Gavotte where they are often so short that they are like a triple mordent.

The effort of performing a number of quick shakes must never be allowed to stiffen the hand or arm. The basic note must always be sung. The trilling fingers should move lightly, relying on their rapidity to supply the impetus that gives the effect of brilliancy.

[1] Ex. 2 in Chapter 1 of *Cello Playing of Today*.

Their swiftness of movement tends to make the reiterated trill note fall rather near the basic note. In semitone trills this can be advantageous as in the interests of 'expressive intonation' it is good to use a small semitone on such trills. In whole tone trills, for acoustical reasons it is important to underline the space between the notes: 1–3 should therefore be taken rather than a 1–2 extension. In places where an extension might seem inevitable, for example:

the hand should be closed up immediately the basic note is sounded, before starting to trill.

SHIFTS IN THE LOWER POSITIONS

When students first attempt to move the hand freely throughout the lower register (i.e. from the half to the fourth position inclusive) they often find it difficult to play in tune. Two specific defects could account for this. One is physical, the other might, at least in part, be termed a question of 'mind over matter'.

The former concerns the thumb. Many beginners experience a recurrent tendency to leave it behind when moving the hand into a higher position. This brings the whole arm unit into an awkward angle to the fingerboard and makes it harder for the finger to reach the heart of its note. In addition, it is apt to engender muscular stiffness. At this stage of instrumental development, it should be kept opposite the second finger when shifting up and down the strings.

One can easily trace the reason for this omission. The

most usual way of learning to change positions is by means of preparatory drills in which the index finger slides from a lower to a higher note on the same string and back again. When this can be accomplished with some degree of assurance, notes with other fingers are added to form part of a scale on one string, like:

in which the first finger remains firmly on the string, the focus of the hand's action and of the player's thought.

Such exercises are invaluable in establishing a foundation on which to develop flexibility in the finger-work. However, in the initial effort of moving away from the familiar first position and listening to make sure that the distances from note to note are being satisfactorily achieved, the thumb is often completely forgotten. Drills should therefore also be introduced involving similar shifts with the second finger, as in these it is more natural to concentrate simultaneously on moving the thumb. As a first step take:

then continue:

which should be elaborated into:

and:

before attempting:

and finally:

This last exercise, in which chromatic ornamentation is used over basic notes that form a part of a diatonic scale, provides a test alike for the intonation and the concentration of the player. The first finger should remain on the string, pinning it down and shifting with the second finger. To facilitate the shifts, the hand should be placed so that the fingers point slightly downwards towards the bridge. The third and fourth fingers should be rounded and held close together above the second. Just before the third descends to strike its note, both should be raised a trifle higher while retaining their curved shape. One word of warning: beneficial as these drills can be, if worked too long at a time they can inflame the ball of the fingers. They should be practised for brief periods and reverted to frequently.

The second probable cause for uncertain intonation is a failure to visualize the placing of the fingers in each new position. In the first place, reflexes should be built up to make it easier for the fingers to respond to the dictates of the ear. To ensure this, over-string drills should be worked, involving moving from one position to another while playing an open string.

As the thumb should be in the crook of the neck when playing in the fourth position, this is the easiest to pitch and should therefore be used first when beginning to work at 'jump-shifts':

Next, apply these ideas to the first and second positions:

and then to the first and third:

always testing the G♮ on the D string with the open string G. An effort should be made to memorize the muscular sensations in the arm and hand and the differences in the stopping as the fingers move towards the bridge. Bearing these matters in mind, more drills should be evolved personally, using the widest variety of note-patterns, fingerings and extensions.

In performance, however, something more is needed. It is often necessary to play entire phrases in certain positions, which means that one has to think ahead and study the shape of the hand in relation to individual passages. The fingers often have to be consciously grouped to take in several consecutive notes in one position before leaving another. For instance, even in the relatively simple

Marcello Sonata in G major, at the beginning of both the first and the last movements:

the hand has to jump from closed first position on one string to extended second on another, and from extended third position to closed first. Such cases are typical of many, which can be troublesome to inexperienced players unless the finger groupings are worked out very carefully in advance.

THE MIDDLE REGISTER

Most elementary cellists feel they have taken a big step forward when they first participate in some form of ensemble. However, they are apt to become frustrated if notes have to be omitted because they are too high for them to play without preliminary practice. Adult beginners, should therefore start learning to find their way about the middle register (positions V–VII inclusive) as soon as a reasonable measure of security has been attained in the lower positions.

They will immediately encounter a new problem. The thumb, having reached the crook of the neck in the fourth position, can no longer travel up and down with the hand. From the fifth position upwards the rest of the unit has to move about on its own. (See p. 42.)

This factor, together with the smaller stopping in the

middle and upper registers, brings a change in the system of fingering. It is no longer advisable to use the little finger when playing a whole tone above the second finger. 1–2–3 should be applied, whether the note groupings consist of three semitones, such as:

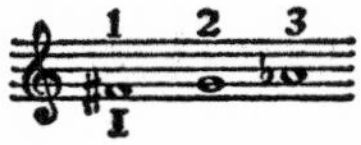

cover a tone and a half as in:

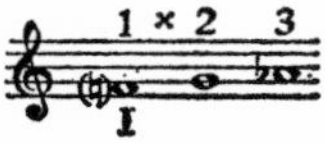

or:

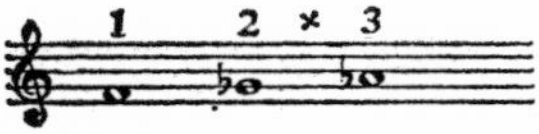

or are made up of two whole tones, like:

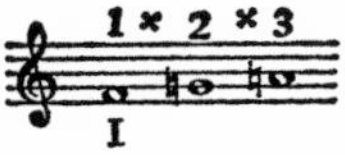

The placing of the hand varies in each position and is influenced by the distribution of tones and semitones in individual passages. In the fifth position it is often virtually impossible to keep it pointing towards the bridge when a whole tone falls between the second and third fingers. Moreover the bigger spacing from note to note compared to that in the sixth and seventh positions makes it the most awkward to handle at the outset. In the sixth position the hand unit is automatically turned more to the side, away from the thumb. This makes the placing more comfortable, but when playing two consecutive whole tones:

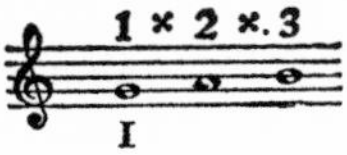

the third finger has to be almost straight while the second is rounded and the first extended backwards. In the seventh position the hand is so far up the fingerboard that some players have to slip the thumb on to the side of the crook before they can reach it. The smaller distances between the notes, however, should eventually make it the easiest to play in tune, particularly in the following note-grouping:

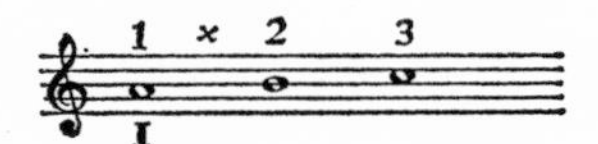

The index finger has the vital function of providing a feeling of stability in each position. Technical development in this register should therefore begin with training it to find its notes on the A string:

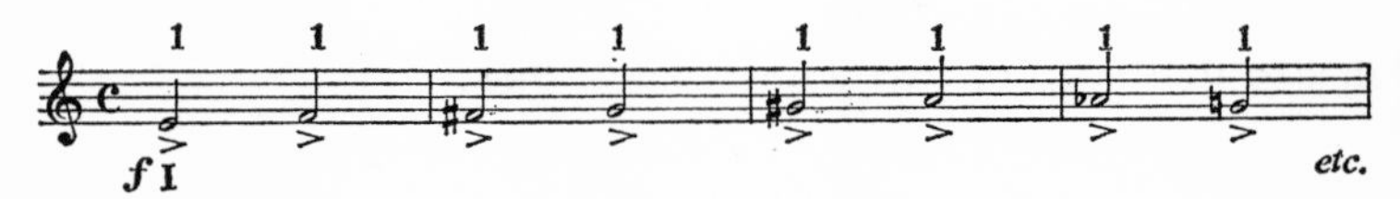

starting from the familiar fourth position. These notes should also be practised returning, after each, to the E:

but readers should again be reminded that these drills should be limited to a few moments at a time, to avoid inflaming the finger tip (see pp. 24, 25, and 76).

Next, take simple sequences moving up the cello chromatically, each bar starting with the first finger *which should never leave the string*. Begin with the easiest, where a whole tone is followed by a semitone and all the fingers point downwards:

Note that the 1–2–3 fingering can already be applied for this note grouping in the fourth position. Gradually increase the speed and alter the order of the tones. Ultimately treat this as an exercise for swift, strong finger articulation:

In note patterns containing a whole tone above the second finger, the hand pointing should generally be squared with the string and the fourth position should be fingered 1–2–4 to prevent straining the third finger. The distribution of intervals in the following will introduce a different way of shifting the hand up a semitone for the next basic first finger note:

Where there are consecutive whole tones, a rhythm should be chosen for the finger drill that will allow enough time on the last note to relax the hand after each extension:

Diatonic note patterns should be worked to develop

flexibility in varying the finger placing. They usually bring different intervals between the fingers in each position. For example, take:

To accustom the hand and arm to shift to and from the lower positions and the middle register, exercises can be made up on the lines of:

amplified little by little to include all types of note-grouping in both registers. They should start on various notes in either the first three positions or in half position. Before leaving the lower note the finger should be pointed downwards ready for the shift. The forearm unit, including the elbow, must be high enough to allow the hand to travel smoothly up the string without colliding with the side of the cello.

RECURRENT WEAKNESSES

So many details are involved in establishing the basis of a sound technique on the cello that it is hardly surprising if less experienced students find it difficult to incorporate them simultaneously. Consequently until the rudiments of good bowing, hand placing and finger articulation have become more or less subconscious, it is necessary to be constantly on the alert. Even after reaching that stage, one has to guard against recurrent weaknesses.

The temperament of the individual player is important here. Some have so little confidence that on approaching something new their muscles tighten up. Others imagine that once they have mastered the elementary precepts of 'fingerboard geography' and legato bowing they are ready to go ahead and play. Each has to find a middle way, striving respectively to dare more and be more self-critical. It is a question of learning to do, listen, and think at the same time.

Certain details are personal. Take bowing. Each hand has its own shape. It is therefore almost impossible to make a hard and fast rule about the rounding (if any) of the fingers on the frog when the hand pulls away from the nut on a down bow. Some players have such long fingers that contact through the 'cushions' can only be obtained if they are more curved than might normally be advocated. In extreme cases, when approaching the nut, the wrist should be held somewhat higher than might in general be considered advisable, to allow the middle fingers freedom of action. No matter how long the fingers may be, the tips should never hang down below the frog.

It is a common failing for the bow to skid about the strings without the player being aware of it. In particular it tends to move in the direction of the fingerboard, as if it were automatically attracted towards the left hand. Unless this is done purposely, to procure certain specific effects, it indicates a lack of bow control. To maintain the position of the stroke parallel with the bridge on every string and at all speeds, one should elaborate on the full-length bow drill quoted on page 6. If it is also extended to cover all four strings and practised with shorter strokes:

it will likewise accustom players to using a smaller movement in the upper arm and a larger one from the elbow to the wrist when performing a series of sectional strokes. It should be worked both near the centre of the bow and from middle to point.

Another recurrent defect frequently encountered is the complete neglect of the third and fourth fingers when they are not needed for immediate action. This affects both hands. When pulling out on a down bow the index finger draws the bow while the second finger and thumb steady the stroke. The other fingers should be helping them, but they often slip off the nut and the little finger lies on the top of the stick. It will thus be forced to shift before it is in place on the frog, ready to push inwards on the up stroke, which is its vital role in bowing. Similarly in the left hand, when several successive notes are enunciated by the first or second fingers, the third and fourth often drop below the level of the string. This again means an unnecessary and often awkward movement to raise them in time to articulate their coming notes from above. Moreover, it prevents their weight being used to reinforce that of the finger vibrating the note.

With the right hand, bowing drills employed alternately at each end of the bow (see p. 7) should set things right. To combat this tendency in the left hand, one should work exercises such as:

which can in addition be used as a vibrato drill. These should be worked on each set of strings in turn and in every position in the lower register. Afterwards they should also be played allegro.

A smear or a break of tone frequently occurs when shifting up and down the cello in a melodic scale passage unless the hand weight is purposefully concentrated on the finger playing the note immediately before the change of position. Exercises to combat this trouble can be combined with those for accustoming the hand to move freely between closed and extended position. For instance, take:

which can be applied in most minor keys. Such drills should likewise counteract any tendency to jerk the hand when shifting from one position to another. In addition, it helps to renew a sense of co-ordination between the hands. The best results are generally obtained by working it with frequent changes of rhythm and key.

Intonation, always a special difficulty for cellists (see pp. 19–23), is particularly vulnerable after an open string. To tone up the ear and strengthen the fingers simultaneously, players should practise a few notes of an over-string chromatic scale:

Finally, before ending a practising session, take a familiar piece, preferably one that introduces easy shifts, and work it with vibrato. If time is short only play a few phrases each day (and not always the same ones!). The aim should be to 'make music' using the technical knowledge already acquired to help to achieve these ends.

PART FOUR

Pizzicato for Cellists

I. *BASIC ELEMENTS*

THERE ARE almost as many varieties of pizzicato as there are of bowings. The subject is therefore a wide one. Strangely enough, however, it is discussed comparatively rarely.

Some teachers encourage pupils to play a stopped note by plucking the string with the index finger of the right hand at their very first lesson. This has the advantage of forcing the beginner to hold the note firmly to the fingerboard and so obtain real sound, whereas when trying, initially, to bow a fingered note noise can be produced regardless of a lack of finger pressure. Thus, it is argued, the use of pizzicato can help to develop strength in the left hand from the start.

On this assumption, the early introduction of pizzicato can be welcomed as a temporary expedient. It must, however, be recognized as such. Otherwise elementary players tend to consider that it simply consists of pulling the string to one side and releasing it again, and, if they can do this, think they have 'learnt pizzicato'!

Pizzicato is governed by many of the same factors as bowing. Just as the bow should be pulled forward and outward to reach the point, so should the arm make a similar movement as the finger plucks the string on a fairly slow forte pizzicato note, such as often occurs in orchestral parts. As with bowed tone, nuance depends mainly on adapting the length of this arm movement and adjusting the contact place of the right hand on the string. To produce full sonority a large sweep of the arm should be employed and the pizzicato effected near the top of the fingerboard. In quiet passages the arm and finger action should be smaller and the string be set in motion farther away from the bridge—that is to say, rather closer to the note played by the left hand.

Whether performing loudly or softly, additional intensity

should be supplied by the left-hand vibrato. It is a mistake to think that because pizzicato carries so clearly it can vitalize and colour the tone entirely on its own. Vibrato has such a compelling influence on the tonal texture that there will always be a change of timbre on an unstopped note unless the left hand continues to vibrate *over* the open strings as and after they are plucked by the fingers of the right hand. On short pizzicato notes followed by a rest, the resonance can be halted by touching the strings lightly with the flat of the hand.

Pizzicato usually needs both a finger (and/or thumb) movement and an arm movement, short or long, executed simultaneously. The speed, length, and proportion of both depends on the tempo, character, and dynamism of the individual passage. On accented notes that should ring out strongly, one should pull out with the whole arm unit, making use, in particular, of the section from the elbow to the knuckles. Generally, however, a smaller action is required and the finger does most of the work.

In applying this technique, begin by taking the two lower octaves of G major scale or the first three octaves of C major and practise them pizzicato. First treat them as if written:

imagining that each note is being stroked by a full down bow. Vibrate constantly and experiment until finding the best place on the string where the plucking finger will give the clearest emission of tone. This will most likely need frequent adjustment, as it will be found that the tone has to be focused, as in bowing, if uniformity is to be obtained on all parts of the instrumental compass. The higher up the string the left hand is, the nearer to the end of the fingerboard the right hand's contact should be made.

Next, without changing the metronomic beat or varying the quantity or quality of the tone, work the scale twice as quickly, two notes to a bar. Analyse the effect that the new speed has on the length of the arm movement. Double the time again so that there would now be four notes in a bar. At this tempo nearly all the action should be coming from the fingers and wrist: the thumb can remain lightly touching, or in close proximity to, the side of the fingerboard which will steady the hand as its movements become more rapid.

The scales should also be practised as if written with different expression marks. Start with either:

or:

and make long tonal gradations from the lowest note to the highest and back again so that *ff* or *pp* are reached, respectively, at the top and *pp* and *ff* on returning to the bottom note. Make sure that the crescendos are continuous: never allow them to progress in a series of sudden spurts. Then try shorter nuances, for instance:

Likewise, play one note loudly and the next softly, always listening and analysing the means needed to produce the sound desired.

CHANGING FROM 'ARCO' TO 'PIZZ'

Students who have trouble in changing quickly and neatly from 'arco' to 'pizz.' and vice versa should practise specialized drills to adjust the grip of the fingers on the frog. It is simplest to apply these first in two-octave scales, played:

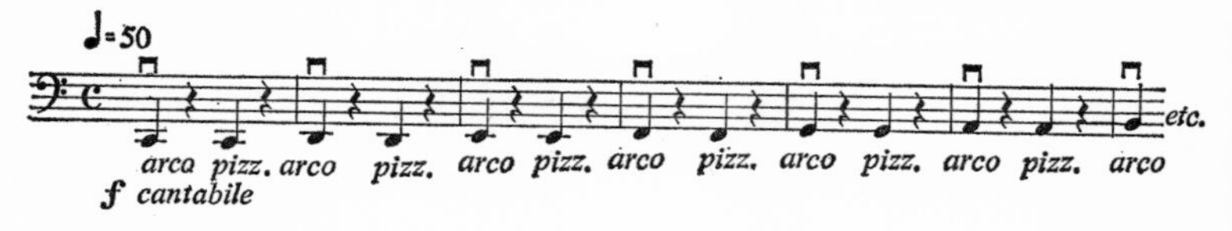

In order to obtain a clear tone in both 'arco' and 'pizz.', a wide sweep of the arm will be needed. This means that the bow will have to return from 'point' to 'nut' position in the air during the rests. While this movement is in progress, prepare for playing pizzicato by curling the second, third and fourth fingers inwards into the palm of the hand. This draws the nut round and changes the entire position of the bow so that the hairs, instead of being more or less parallel with the ground, are facing the performer. In the meantime the index finger should leave its place on the stick and the thumb simultaneously disengage itself from the frog. The finger will thus be ready to pluck the string, while the thumb can be placed on the side of the fingerboard to steady the hand during the pizzicato. The wrist, which bends naturally in sympathy with the finger movement, will bring the hand almost automatically into position for plucking the string.

This process should be used in reverse when returning to 'arco' after a plucked note. The second, third, and fourth fingers have to straighten themselves, rolling the bow over until it regains its original angle to the floor. The thumb and first finger should be in place on the nut before the straightening action is completed. It might almost be said that the finger movement is in two parts: a small preliminary turn of the three fingers on the frog while the first finger and the thumb are still reacting to their work in the pizzicato, and a more definite straightening of all the fingers as soon as the first and the thumb are in position for bowing. (The word 'straightened' must be treated with reserve here—the fingers should rarely be quite straight in bowing—but it is difficult to find a more suitable term to clarify their movement.)

When these manipulations can be accomplished smoothly *over* the strings, try them out in the scales already quoted. Gradually quicken the pace, omit the rests, and use different rhythms, such as:

remembering that the more rapidly the notes follow each other, the less bow will be needed for the 'arco' to correspond with the shorter arm action in the pizzicato.

Experiment next by using up bow instead of down bow. When a plucked note is followed by an up bow starting at the tip, much concentration may be required before it can be enunciated clearly at precisely the right moment. This is most noticeable on open strings. Unless they are consciously 'stopped' (see p. 90), their tone tends to ring on some time after the pizzicato has been terminated. To combat this difficulty, work the scales on the following lines:

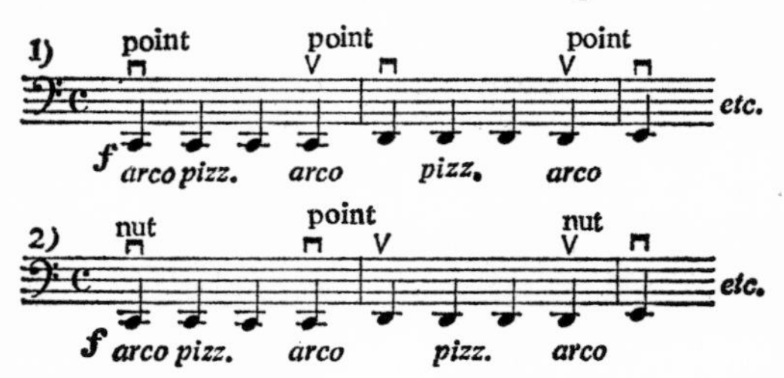

Exercises based on open chords covering all four strings should be added:

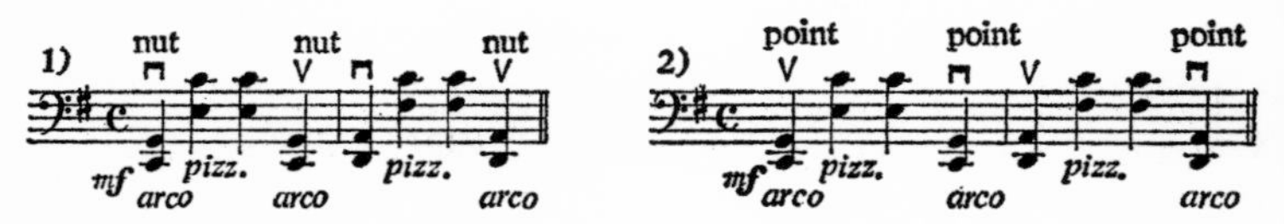

First work example 1, using very little bow and keeping to the section near the nut. When the movements can be accomplished with ease, try the bowings in example 2, playing at or near the point. The pizzicato chords in double stopping should be plucked with the first finger and the thumb, the former on the A string and the latter on the D. Their actions must be made to synchronize exactly. The arm can help by moving slightly upwards and outwards after the notes are enunciated.

The drills should also be reversed:

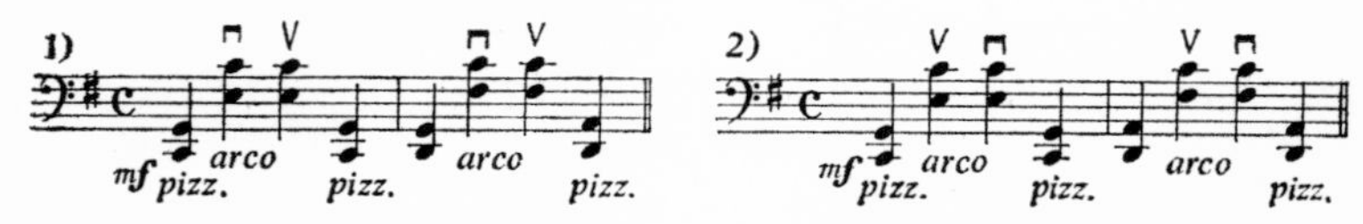

The thumb and the first finger, which are now used respectively for plucking the C and G strings, can be supported as they leave their notes by a sympathetic arm movement. This, however, should never be so wide that the hand

and wrist are not in position on the bow, ready in advance for the coming arco notes. One must also be very careful that the bow returns to its correct angle for playing on the upper strings before coming down to strike them after the pizzicato.

DIVERSE TYPES OF PIZZICATO

The choice of which type of pizzicato should be used in specific cases is largely a matter of common sense applied to the indications of the composer. The character of the music has to be taken into account as well as the speed of the passage, the length of the notes and the volume and texture of the tone. Chords and double stopping call for the greatest variety of treatment but in the first instance the fingers and thumb have to be trained to pluck one string at a time.

This 'single string' pizzicato is the form most frequently found in classical chamber music and simple orchestral parts. Cellists usually prefer to perform it with the index finger but there is no definite rule. In any case the second finger should always be prepared to take over if necessary.

An example occurs of this in Beethoven's 'Archduke' trio, Op. 97, where a long episode in pizzicato starts softly and mounts to a climax. If the first finger is used throughout, the majority of players find it is practically impossible to preserve sufficient reserves of strength to produce a ringing forte on the final notes. The accepted device is to change to the second finger between the earlier phrases during the long crescendo and so rest the first finger, returning to it after a few bars so that it is in action towards the close, where the most power is needed.

In rapid passages or very soft rhythmic music (such as the Scherzo of the Fauré G minor piano quartet) the arm movement can be virtually eliminated. Consequently, although it is good to back up the finger action with that of the arm whenever the tempo and volume of tone permit, the fingers should also be taught to act on their own. The thumb can then remain on the side of the fingerboard or, when plucking the lower strings, just above it. This gives the fingers a feeling of stability that is particularly welcome when moving rapidly. (See p. 91.)

To obtain facility in the fingers, work over-string exercises using scale patterns. Start by:

plucking the string with the first finger. Contact should be made by the side of the 'cushion' of the top phalanx rather than on its tip. This roughly corresponds to the place normally used by the index finger of the left hand when playing B on the A string in the first position in this scale.

Listen consciously to the regularity of the rhythm and the quality of the tone. As regards the latter, the vitality introduced by the percussive fingers of the left hand enunciating their notes plays an important part. A similar spark should be felt in the finger plucking the string. Efforts to develop this, however, must never be allowed to stiffen the hand. Increase the speed slightly each day until the drills can be performed as if written:

and lengthen them to cover three octaves instead of two.

When this exercise can be played neatly with the first finger, work it with the second. To begin with it may react more slowly and feel rather clumsy, due in part to its extra length. It must also be remembered that most cellists instinctively pluck the string with the index finger, not with the second. To acquire equal freedom of action with both, in addition to practising such drills exclusively with the middle finger, students should vary their approach, playing one bar with one finger and the next with another. Later change fingers after every four notes and ultimately after every two.

Drills on these lines and those suggested on pages 91 to 93 should likewise be worked with the thumb. In their relationship to the general movement of the arm unit, thumb pizzicato might be compared to playing up bow whereas finger pizzicato resembles playing down bow. At first the former may seem the harder to accomplish because the fingers cannot steady the hand for the thumb in the same way that the thumb can for the fingers, but with practice it should not present any serious difficulties.

The thumb can produce greater flexibility of tone than the finger. This is probably best revealed in the slow movement of Brahms's F major sonata, Op. 99, where the cellist has to provide a steady, telling counterpoint to the theme given out by the pianist. As the cello has the moving part, these pizzicatos in the first two bars set the atmosphere for the whole 'Adagio'. The enunciation must be completely regular, controlled but never rigid. The vibrato must carry the tone between the strokes of the thumb so that one note moves towards the next, inevitably and melodically. This can be effected far more naturally if the string is plucked from *below* with the thumb rather than from *above* with the fingers. For similar reasons a thumb pizzicato can often be extremely effective in chamber music, for instance in the beats given out by the second cello in the first section of the slow movement of the Schubert C major String Quintet, Op. 163.

The thumb itself has to be firm and its movement backed by the arm action, the extent of which varies according to the dynamic strength required. For instance, at the climax of the Brahms Adagio, thumb pizzicato can be employed with excellent effect on the A string if it is directed with a forward, outward swing of the lower arm from the elbow downwards. Despite its tonal advantages, however, the use of thumb pizzicato should be reserved for special occasions.

PIZZICATO CHORDS

There seems to be virtually no limit to the diversity of effects which can be obtained by plucking two or more strings together, either simultaneously or to give the impression of a broken chord. Contemporary composers are still experimenting in this field with increasing audacity. Complicated feats in pizzicato, however, even more than those in bowing, instinctively call for individual treatment and nearly every expert achieves a personal style and mastery. The subject will therefore be discussed here in a general way, the object being to suggest some logical means through which students can work things out for themselves.

Take an orchestral part where two notes on adjacent strings have to be plucked together. They cannot always be performed 'divisi' as there may be an uneven number of cellists, one of whom has to play both notes to preserve the balance. Moreover similar pizzicatos often occur in chamber music, where there is only one instrumentalist to each desk. These pizzicatos are frequently inherent to the rhythmic design of the music and recur repeatedly. Thus, all embryo cellists should train the hands to perform them with controlled efficiency.

The strings should be plucked with a kind of pincer action of the thumb (on the lower note) and the index finger (on the higher string). Their movements must synchronize absolutely. As contact is made with the strings, a forward and upward swing of the arm unit from the elbow will help to vitalize the sonority. In the fortes the upper arm should be used to reinforce the swing of the lower arm whenever time permits, but in soft passages little more than a wrist movement is needed.

The main difficulty lies in developing sufficient facility in the thumb to match that of the finger, usually the more pliable of the two. This is essential if the notes are to sound at exactly the same instant. In the preliminary stages it is often necessary to combat a tendency of the first finger to strike slightly in advance of the thumb. Bearing this in mind, start experimenting in the two lower octaves of scales in thirds and sixths. Work them slowly first:

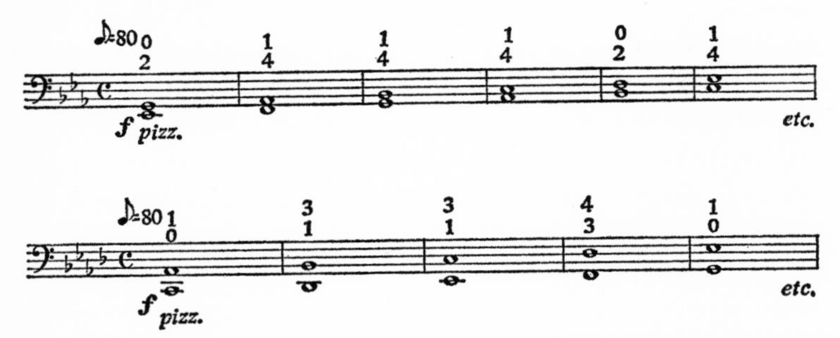

then gradually quicken the tempo. Next treat the scales as if they were written:

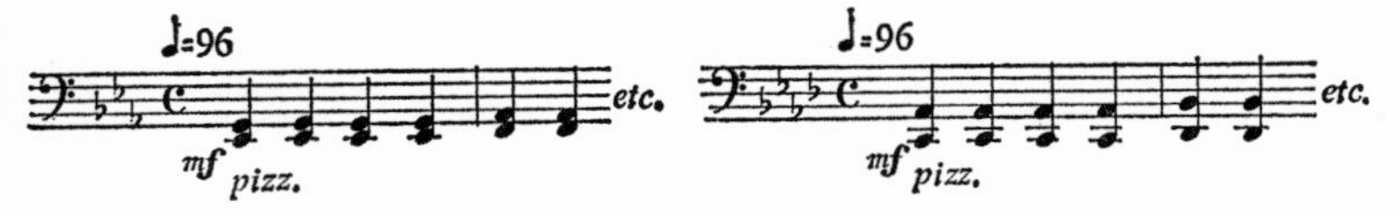

followed, as proficiency is gained, by changing notes on both the first and third beats of each bar.

Pizzicato chords vary according to their context. Some should be stroked from below, the arm action resembling that of an up bow, others from above, where its swing can be likened to a down bow. Certain composers, such as Gordon Jacob in his Rondino, use the sign

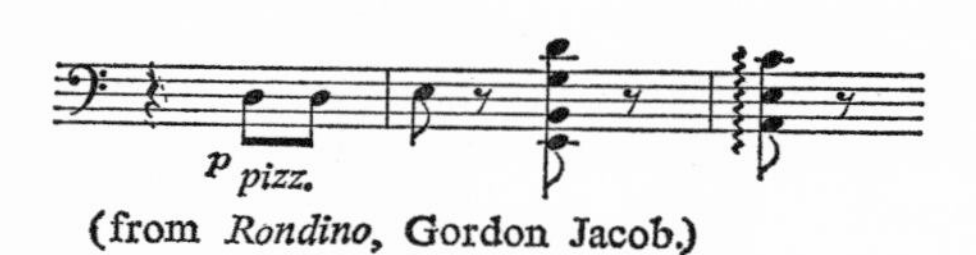

(from *Rondino*, Gordon Jacob.)

to indicate that an open chord is needed. This normally means that it should be stroked from the bass upwards. However, similar effects can also be dictated by the character of the music, as we find in the Fauré *Sicilienne*, where the almost rigid thumb should be swept forward smoothly over the strings, its movement so well controlled that a delicate, gracious tone can be produced. Contact with the string should be made with the flat of the 'cushion' and the arm action planned to enable the thumb to touch each string rather nearer the top of the fingerboard than on the preceding string.

The triumphant pizzicato chord at the close of Frank Bridge's *Melody* requires a brilliant tone. This can best be produced if it is played from the top, downwards. The bow should be gripped in the palm of the hand by the thumb while all four fingers, placed so close to each other that they might be glued together, sweep diagonally across the strings, backed by a firm, wide arm movement. Some 'down bow' pizzicato chords can likewise be played using the second, third and fourth fingers as a single unit to strike the upper strings and the thumb to pluck the lowest one while the index finger holds the bow.

A third type of pizzicato chord involves plucking three or four strings simultaneously by different digits. There is an example of this in the last bar of the Scherzo of Brahms's C major Piano Trio, Op. 87. Where only three strings are used it is generally best to take the thumb for the bottom note, the first finger for the middle one and the second for the highest. Where four strings are needed the third finger should pluck the A string.

Plucked chords of all kinds can be worked in three- and four-string drills like:

Practise them first fairly softly as open chords, stroked with the thumb from below. Afterwards pluck them more loudly with the fingers from above. Later, play each chord, twice, plucked once with the thumb and once with the fingers. Next use separate digits. Finally experiment by taking the three kinds of pizzicato alternately:

gradually increasing the speed of the chords.

COMBINING DIFFERENT PIZZICATO TECHNIQUES

Combining different types of pizzicato so that they can either be used together or in extremely rapid succession, requires great technical skill. Its application is determined by the demands of the music and, to some extent, by the physical formation of the individual hand.

Take, for instance, the guitar-like effect, where a series of split chords are employed to point and underline the rhythm. This occurs in different forms in countless works. When three strings are covered the note grouping often consists of a low note plucked alone followed by two higher notes plucked together, as for example:

and:

where both thumb and finger pizzicato can be applied. Where four strings are involved, the notes are frequently plucked two and two with the thumb and the first finger although sometimes two of the strings are sounded together and two separately. Other variations include plucking the C string alone, generally from below with the thumb, and the three upper strings simultaneously with the fingers. (See p. 101.)

First practise exercises on three strings. Any progression can be used, such as the following adapted freely from the Prelude of the Bach G major unaccompanied suite:

etc.

Start by plucking the lower string by itself and the other two together, playing each chord twice. Then reverse this: begin with the top note played alone followed by the lower notes plucked simultaneously. Next, experiment with the fingerings of the pizzicato, using every reasonable combination. Also work it with a variety of nuances and dynamics. At performance there may not be much time between the notes, so the crescendos and accents should be chiefly made by increasing the speed of the plucking movement. In a forte, approach the string from a little further above it and place the hand nearer the end of the fingerboard than would be appropriate when a softer tone is required. Even if a specific finger is in constant use the thumb need not be kept on the side of the fingerboard when playing louder as this could hamper the action of the hand.

When applying this technique on all four strings, use can be made of the progression suggested on page 101. Treat the chords as freely as possible, dividing each in every conceivable way. Also change the time values and rhythmic patterns very frequently to prevent the movements from becoming automatic.

When first studying passages from works involving over-string pizzicato try to think of every group of notes as a chord. Pluck it with a single sweep of the hand, either from above with the fingers or from below with the thumb. Make sure that the fingers of the left hand are in place on all the notes before starting the pizzicato. Even when the passages are later played as printed, whenever practicable the fingers of the left hand should be on all the notes of the group in advance, before the first of them is plucked. This will provide a much needed sense of stability.

The essential part played in pizzicato by the vitality and percussive strength of the fingers of the left hand should never be disregarded. It is evident alike in the constant background of vibrato which helps to carry the tone from note to note, and, even more directly, when two notes have to be played by the same pizzicato 'twang'. Probably the best known example of this latter occurs in the famous episode from the Finale of the Brahms F major sonata, but it was actually introduced earlier in a simpler form in the theme of the second movement of Mendelssohn's D major sonata:

It is advisable here to use the second finger of the right hand to pluck the string rather than the first, because its tip is broader and produces a better quality of tone. The third finger E on the grace note should be struck firmly and the forearm move quickly to the F♯ glissando. The plucking of the first finger D should suffice to set the string in action but if the result is not satisfactory one can pluck both the D and the E.

Twentieth-century composers often demand the enunciation of successive notes on the same string in different positions during a single pizzicato stroke. This is accomplished by using the weight and intensity of the vibrant left hand to vitalize the finger as it shifts rapidly about the string. The influence of the vibrato can be so great that if the vibrant left hand moves downwards *over* the strings after they have been plucked, it gives the impression of a chromatic run. Ravel in his *Duo* procures some colourful effects by these means.

Left-hand pizzicato is sometimes introduced to sound notes on one string while the bow is playing on another.

This device, once solely associated with virtuoso works such as Kodály's solo sonata, Op. 8, is now often found in chamber music. To prepare for it, practise long-sustained bowed notes on each string in turn, accompanying them by plucked notes played by various fingers on other strings. In so doing, be careful never to disturb the smoothness of the tone.

Pizzicato is a natural element in cello technique, not merely an amusing adjunct to it. It should often be graceful, sometimes dramatic and occasionally grotesque. If at times its main object seems to be to underline humour, one must remember that Brahms, who employed it in so many different ways, chose it to supply the basic pulse and the climactic power in one of the most profound pages of our literature.

PART FIVE

Reflections and Reminders

ACCENT ON QUALITY

SOME YEARS ago, Britain was given an historic example of quality in music by the superb performance of the two lone trumpeters who sounded, respectively, the 'Last Post' and 'Reveille' at the state funeral of Sir Winston Churchill. Both were impeccable, alike in tone, phrasing and timing. Their effect was to sum up wordlessly in moving simplicity a nation's pride and gratitude.

These trumpet solos gave musicians much cause for reflection. They held a grandeur that will not soon be forgotten, and many who, on the day, were stirred by their impact felt impelled to try to discover how their example could be applied personally, to engender a greater demand for quality in their own endeavours.

Specifically, from the instrumentalist's point of view, their mastery must have made sensitive listeners realize afresh the complete satisfaction that can be derived from purity of tone and style allied to that hint of great-heartedness so fitting to the occasion. The sonority was neither harsh nor shrill, yet it always had substance. For cellists this was perhaps the most important object lesson of all.

The distinctive fundamental character of the cello is its warm, deep tone. It can be compared with the joint ranges of singers in the bass, baritone, and 'Heldentenor' groups. Other additions should be superimposed later but it is from these virile beginnings that prospective players should work.

Basic technique should be taught with this in view, so that pupils will know from the first by what means this quality can be produced and learn to accustom the ear to demand it. Once a feeling for a round, focused forte or mezzoforte tone is established it can be softened by lightening the bow arm, using less bow, playing farther from the bridge, and so on.

In the early stages, however, its quality (as opposed to its quantity) should remain unchanged.

Some students practise lightly, almost tonelessly, because they claim that it helps them to hear the intonation more clearly. The idea of working quietly is good, in that it eliminates extraneous sound and prevents players from being carried away emotionally too soon and consequently ceasing to be sufficiently self-critical. This latter defect can result in playing slightly but persistently out of tune.

Unfortunately, however, it also has some obvious disadvantages. If cellists seldom produce a full, glowing tone it will reduce their desire for it. Furthermore, it is apt to lead them to concentrate solely on one aspect of instrumental development instead of stimulating a dual sense of hearing which simultaneously encourages the demand for a tonal texture that matches the purity sought in the intonation, a texture that can ultimately be so well adjusted that even in a pianissimo it has substance.

This does not mean that students should consistently work forte. Through force of circumstances some have to practise in rather cramped quarters or in places where they feel they cannot play out freely for fear of disturbing their neighbours. At the other extreme very resonant rooms tend to overamplify the tone, which gives inexperienced performers an exaggerated idea of its power and volume. While it is exhilarating to play occasionally under such acoustical conditions it is rarely wise to accustom the ear to them in daily practice. Again it is a question of listening for quality.

When working over the full instrumental compass students should be actively aware of the differences of finger and bow pressure required in the various registers. Not only do the lower strings need greater percussive effort in the finger articulation than the A and D, but as the left hand nears the top of the fingerboard the bow has to cut across the strings at a changed place and angle. This sometimes involves an adjustment of the arm weight.

It is interesting to note that prior to important solo appearances certain master cellists evolve double stopping drills on adjacent strings, covering two octaves. To suggest a simple example, take:

and use the rhythms given in Cossmann's double trills. Begin in the first register, then without stopping, shift the hand up an octave, and afterwards two, returning it in between to the original position. There should be no change of strings and the same quality of tone should be produced and preserved throughout. Advanced students adopting this drill should find it invaluable in developing a controlled, vital tone on all parts of the instrument.

TO EXTEND OR NOT TO EXTEND

In many instances the 1–2–3 system of fingering is now almost universally recognized as having superseded the more conservative 1–3–4 even in the lower registers of the cello. The cases in question consist, specifically, of note groups covering a tone and a half in the same position, in which the whole tone falls after the first finger and the semitone lies between the higher notes. There is an example of this in the following phrase from Max Bruch's *Kol Nidrei*:

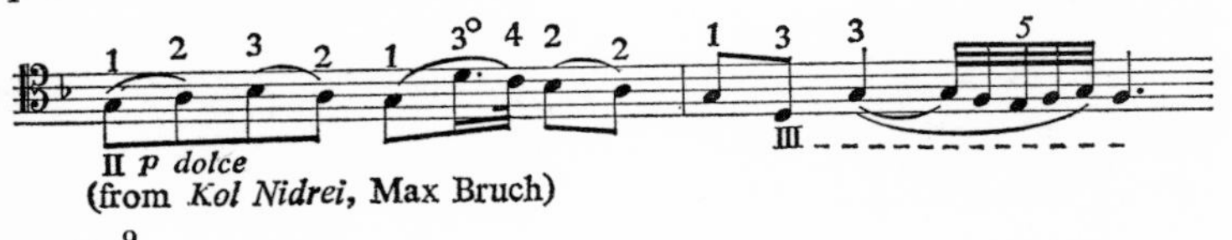

(from *Kol Nidrei*, Max Bruch)

The advantages are twofold. By avoiding the frequent use of the short fourth finger it enables the hand pointing to be more natural. By utilizing the attraction between the second and third fingers which share the same tendon to play the semitone, it makes it easier to perform this small, sensitive interval with good intonation.

As regards tone, however, a compact hand can sometimes be extremely helpful, particularly in early days at the cello, because it brings the weight of each finger more normally behind whichever one is enunciating the note. Experienced cellists counteract any such difficulty by consciously—and eventually subconsciously—closing up the fingers each time after they have been stretched out, providing that the time factor permits. At the beginning this demands a considerable mental effort, without which these fingerings, instead of making the hand feel more comfortable, could stiffen the whole unit.

A complication is liable to arise from the fact that cellists often do not understand exactly *when* the fingering should be applied. In determining this, players should ask themselves a simple question: 'Is there a reasoned and logical need for an extension?' If there is, employ the 1–2–3 fingering; if not, take advantage of a compact hand.

To clarify this, examine and compare the note placing in the first two octaves of C major and D major scales, each of which is in the first position:

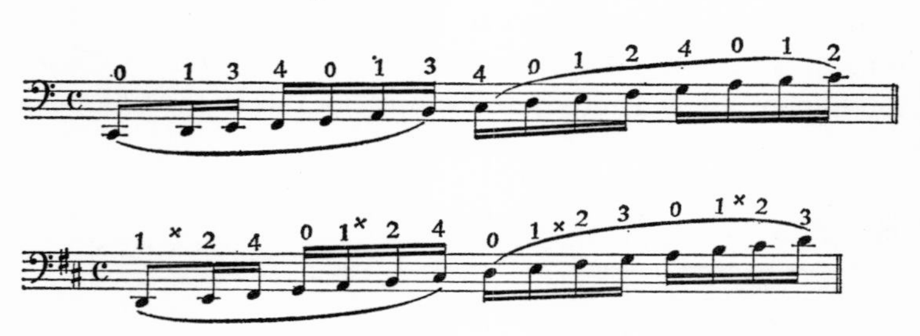

In C major the semitones come between E and F, B and C. At a first glance it might seem as if the 1–2–3 system is indicated for the lower octave, but in the next octave the semitones fall between the first and second fingers. That means the hand must be closed on the upper strings in order to play these notes in tune. If the hand was to be opened out for the 1–2–3 fingering in the first octave it would therefore be necessary to change its placing (including that of the thumb which should be opposite the second finger) while playing the open string D. This would be far more complicated than beginning with 0–1–3–4 on the lower strings and keeping the fingers in their compact position throughout.

In the scale of D major the situation is different. The hand must be extended on the bottom strings otherwise it would be impossible to play the groups of two whole tones—D to F♯ and A to C♯—accurately in the same position. Furthermore, in the second octave the semitone lies just below the highest of the fingered notes on each string, so it would be superfluous to close up the hand. There are also strong reasons for keeping it open and playing the G and D with the third finger, in that it eliminates an unnecessary change of finger pointing which can be awkward when playing quickly. It also brings the hand into the best placing for ultimately continuing up the A string to play the third and fourth octaves.

For this latter reason it is advisable in all major scales other than C to take the 1–2–3 fingering on the top notes of the second octave. The limited length of the little finger has the effect of pulling the hand round into squared placing when it plays the tonic above the sharpened leading note. Consequently it should be avoided whenever possible in ascending scale passages on the same string. It will make the slide far smoother and more certain if the fingers point downwards towards the bridge before leaving a lower position than if the higher registers are approached from 'squared' placing.

Nevertheless, it is often good to take 1–3–4 on the lower strings. As the fingers are farther away from the wrist and elbow than on the A and D strings, the spaces from note to note on the G and C appear greater which makes the extensions more of an effort. Moreover, the help given by the use of a compact hand placing in fairly rapid cantabile passages should never be disregarded. Thus in the following episodes from the Preludes of the G major:

(from Prelude of Suite
No. 1 in G, Bach)

and D minor:

(from Prelude of Suite
No. 2 in D minor, Bach)

Bach solo suites, it can be strongly recommended, although in both movements there are many places which are most comfortable fingered 1–2–3. Readers should experiment for themselves.

These pointers should give players a little guidance so that they can work out the problems of when and when not to extend. Each hand is different so there can be no hard and fast rules. The question of bone structure has to be considered against the harmonic and melodic background of the music, and the phrasing and character of every work.

MANNERISMS

Mannerisms can usually be traced to facets in the personality of the individual player. They are not necessarily harmful, in fact some can be endearing—historic examples of this were provided by Fritz Kreisler and Artur Schnabel. Frequently, however, they are responsible for musical and technical defects and if so, immediate steps should be taken to eradicate them.

Bad habits that can lead to mannerisms should of course be guarded against from the outset. For example, many inexperienced cellists have an erroneous instinct that causes them to let the third and fourth fingers of the left hand hang down below the side of the fingerboard while playing a first or second finger note in the lower register. This habit tends to persist, making it difficult to keep all the fingers automatically above the level of the strings (see pp. 84–5).

This elementary fault, if uncorrected, will affect the tone. Students who listen carefully to themselves must be aware of the improvement in its texture when the vibrating finger is backed by the weight of the others grouped above it. Unfortunately some players become so accustomed to the sound of their sonority that they accept it without question. If it displeases them they attribute it, regretfully, to lack of talent or to a mediocre instrument. It is true that very gifted cellists generally have a 'natural' vibrato and so produce beauty of tone more easily. Nevertheless, by training the fingers to group themselves together and to stretch out towards the coming note, it is possible to cultivate a sensitive vibrato that will add quality and colour to the tone, providing that no obstinate habits are interfering with their reflexes.

Although weaknesses of this kind can be contributory factors in cellistic mannerisms they are rarely the main cause of their appearance. As a rule they are associated with temperamental characteristics, particularly with the more advanced instrumentalists. Furthermore, whereas most of them are personal, a few might be termed 'contagious', especially if they are introduced by a player who has a certain prestige among his peers. Once, a top cellist of his year at a famous London music college, who felt rhythm strongly, contracted the unconscious habit of swaying from the hips to the pulse of the music. He led the cello section of the student orchestra: practically all his colleagues temporarily and quite unwittingly developed a similar 'wriggle'.

Another obstinate mannerism prevalent about that time was a grimace made through pulling in the cheeks and the lower jaw. This facial contortion represented the extremes of muscular and psychological tension occasioned by an intense effort of concentration. Nowadays so much emphasis is rightly laid on matters appertaining to relaxation that fewer players are troubled in this way. As with all forms of undue emotional and physical stress (including those which result in heavy breathing or humming) the cure comes through taking full advantage of the breathing spaces provided by the 'commas' in the musical sentences. In some obstinate cases, when practising—never at performance, that would create another irritating mannerism!—cellists might try to smile on reaching such points just as they would flex the finger and arm muscles if they were stiff.

Most concert artists have mannerisms. Some are based on logic. Take two that are typical of Pablo Casals: that of playing with closed eyes and the head facing away from the cello *in order to listen to himself more objectively*, and that of turning the line of his shoulders from left to right and vice versa *so that he can play with complete freedom of action on the outer strings*.

Certain brilliantly talented executants, however, are so

carried away at performance that they throw themselves about constantly. Apart from all else this distracts the attention of the audience. Obviously no player should sit motionless on a chair as if in a straitjacket, but highly charged interpreters should seek some middle way whereby such exaggerations can be curbed. Vitality of expression can then be carried over through well-directed actions of the finger and bow undisturbed by a series of uncontrolled movements that affect the entire upper part of the body. These superfluous gestures may become increasingly noticeable when a professional career is under way. If so, family and friends should give frank warnings whenever such symptoms appear.

With some, these tendencies are apt to have the more serious effect of interfering with the phrasing and distorting the musical line. They can result in jerks that give a false accent after the note has been articulated and lead to an unwanted crescendo on a final note. The subconscious influence of one hand on the other is so great that a sudden, extraneous movement of the left arm can adversely affect the bow distribution. The player may be unaware of this because most mannerisms become like second nature and thus pass unnoticed by the instrumentalist. This makes it harder to correct them.

It can be done, as has been proved, by the exercise of determination and self-control. For the average player, however, 'prevention is better than cure'. Cellists who feel the music deeply should therefore be continually on the alert so that incipient mannerisms are never allowed to assume excessive prominence. They will thus always feel free, physically, to associate themselves with the music and play with intensity and beauty.

'I LACK FACILITY!'

'I lack facility!' This comes as a cry from the heart of many an aspiring cellist. 'It isn't so bad where there is time to think. The slow movements of my sonata seem better but I come to grief in the quick ones. What can I do?'

Rather surprisingly, perhaps, good grounding suitable for slow performance plays an important role in the development of fluency. When striving to play rapidly many actions of the hand and arm are basically the same as when working deliberately, although their application varies as regards degree. Take, for instance the first two octaves of the D♭ major scale:

This is particularly useful to cellists who are learning to shift from one position to another across the strings without jerking. First work the scale very slowly, two notes to a bow, preparing each shift to a higher string by *slipping the thumb back along the neck until it is opposite the first finger instead of the second* while the fourth finger is sounding its E♭, B♭, or A♭. When descending, the thumb should move towards the higher position while the first finger plays its note. Next work the scale an octave, and later two octaves to a bow. Ultimately treat the notes like quick semiquavers. When so doing it will probably be found that there is not time to stretch out the hand fully for the double extensions and that the fingers will have to jump the last portion of the shifts. Nevertheless, if the muscles have been trained to play their part they should soon adapt themselves to the faster movements. As in all scale practice, always be careful that there are no smudges between the notes when changing position.

A further helpful example occurs in the first six notes of the second octave of B♭ major scale, fingered:

which, owing to the consecutive extensions, introduces an awkward note-sequence. Unless the player establishes the habit here of slipping the first finger up the A string towards the second and the third while playing the C and D in the first position, it is extremely difficult to enunciate the E♭ without a break of tone, a smear, or slightly faulty intonation. Without leaving the string the index finger should therefore prepare itself to slide swiftly on to the E♭ from below by approaching the fourth finger as closely as is practicable. Its movements should be practised slowly at the outset but as soon as the hand can be relied upon to shift neatly a faster speed should be attempted. Although this technique is unsuitable for beginners it should, in the end, become virtually instinctive.

In order to gain facility exercises should be worked to train the fingers to come down firmly and rapidly to articulate their notes. Cellists should realize, however, that agility will be of little value if its quest leads to the production of a harsh or unfocused tone, just as the development of strong finger action becomes pointless if the digits are incapable of reaching the heart of their notes. Less experienced students should make certain that they are on the right road by occasionally stopping the bow for a moment when practising a solo, a study or a drill, and continue by sounding the notes solely through the left hand percussion (see pp. 9–10).

In bowing, the terms 'sustained' and 'detached' are often associated respectively with playing slowly and quickly. In this, the similarity of approach underlined in left-hand technique is somewhat less obvious. Even so, unless the bow can be controlled on long notes it is doubtful whether short strokes will be executed entirely successfully. Certainly a fine legato is an essential background in many forms of *detaché*, especially those founded on the pendulum arm motion, that is to say in most types of spiccato or semi-spiccato.

Other kinds of *detaché*, notably those based on a 'staccato' root:

require a quick, biting action of the fingers on the frog. This, together with its subsequent release as the bow is carried inwards or outwards, might be described as an independent element superimposed on the principles laid down for sustained bowing. It can be used to achieve a diversity of effects. Incorporated into scale practice it should likewise help students to master another general factor vital to fluent performance—the perfect co-ordination between the movements of the two hands.

Another admirable means of widening the instrumental horizon and gaining greater freedom in moving about the cello consists of devoting a short time each day to comparatively simple studies. Players should concentrate on the special points that every work is designed to cover, trying to perform it sufficiently well to be able to take a new one after a few days. They should choose études well within their present scope as the plan will fail in its purpose to stimulate agility if it is necessary to spend too long in deciphering the notes.

More advanced cello students could, with advantage, substitute for this project a study of some of the now neglected nineteenth-century teaching concertos. Musically the works of Davidoff, Goltermann, Molique, and Romberg may seem somewhat trite today, but they still have their place in developing virtuosity. Furthermore, when allotted a strictly limited portion of the practising time they can provide an intriguing challenge.

SOME HINTS ON PREPARATION

The word 'preparation' does not refer, here, to the many stages of practising needed before instrumentalists are ready to give of their best at performance. Its scope is more limited and concerns the diverse aspects of thought and technical approaches that can be employed to advantage immediately before starting a work, a movement, a phrase, or an accent. This aspect of preparation is often neglected, the result being that the desired mood is not created until several notes—and sometimes bars—have been played.

Take a seventeenth- or eighteenth-century sonata beginning with a slow movement, such as that by Dr Arne in B♭ major (arr. Harold Craxton):

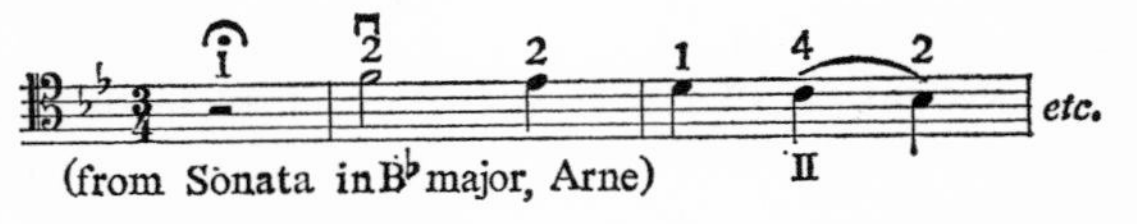

As the pianist strikes the introductory chord the cellist should place the finger on the F and start vibrating in order that the tone will sing directly the bow touches the string. The bow should be carefully arranged on about three-quarters of the hair width, at a reasonable distance from the end of the fingerboard. These simple preliminaries should help to produce the tone quality that will set the atmosphere for the whole movement.

This approach is often applicable in works where the

piano starts before the cello, for instance the Fauré *Elégie*, Max Bruch's *Kol Nidrei*, the first of Schumann's Op. 73 Fantasy Pieces for cello and piano, Mendelssohn's Op. 108, and the slow movement of the Bax Sonatina. It is also useful in certain duo sonatas, like the Beethoven G minor, Op. 5 No. 2, and Brahms E minor, Op. 38, in which both instruments commence together. However, as the works are bound to differ considerably in spirit, the cellist must realize in advance what specific type of vibrato and rate of bow distribution will be required to produce the colour desired at the initial entry.

In the Prelude of the Bach G major solo suite:

the first finger should vibrate the B before the open string G has been played. Advanced cellists are advised to use a light plucking action with the third finger of the left hand on the G: this must synchronize absolutely with the enunciation of the note by the bow and be so well controlled that it does not disturb the vibration of the first finger. The same ideas can be adopted in the opening of Minuet No. 1 and on the chord at the beginning of the Sarabande.

One of the main difficulties in the Allemande:

lies in preventing the chord from disrupting the intensity of the short up beat leading into the longer down beat. The player should *think* the rhythm prior to playing the first note and hear the two Bs which form the melodic line in imagination, as if they were the syllables 'da-DA'. First practise these notes without the chord. When it is subsequently inserted, time it so that its top note, not its bass, falls exactly on to the 'one' of the bar.

Half way through the first part of the Courante in this same suite there is an example of a different preparatory approach useful in achieving co-ordination between the fingers and the bow in phrasing:

(from Courante of Suite No. I in G, Bach)

To produce a clear tone on the B, take advantage of the punctuation which should cause the bow to stop naturally at the end of the G. During this infinitesimal break, shift the left hand quickly into the third position, placing the first finger on the G. Raise the little finger over the B and drop it down at the precise moment that the new phrase should begin. This should be the signal for the bow to move in on its up stroke.

This device can often be used with excellent results. For example, at the beginning of the slow movement of the Sammartini Sonata in G:

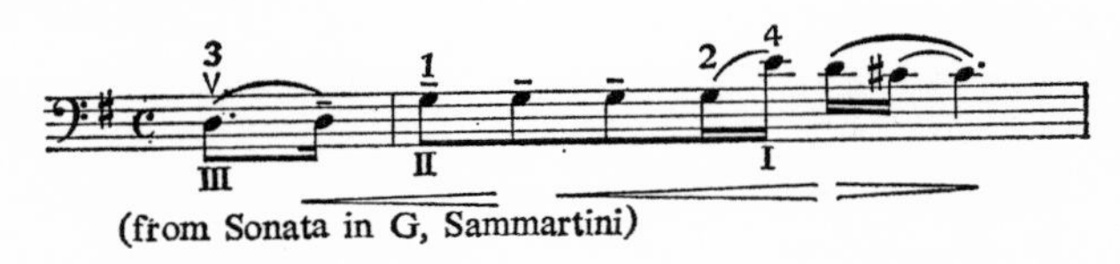

(from Sonata in G, Sammartini)

the index finger should be placed on the *C* and the bow on the string near the point, ready to start the instant the third finger comes down to articulate and sing the D. Other occasions when this technique can be applied include the enunciation of the first note of the 'Quasi Minuetto' movement of the Brahms Op. 38 and the first note of the Allegro in the Boccherini A major sonata.

When an accent is required at the initial cello entry (as in the Brahms Double and the Dvořák concertos) or at the start of a phrase, such as the following from the *Kol Nidrei*:

(from *Köl Nidrei*, Max Bruch)

this procedure can be adopted in reverse. Prepare the left hand with the first finger on its note and the fourth on the same string a tone and a half above it. Make sure that the bow is poised ready to strike. Then pluck the fourth finger backwards and upwards so that it springs back over the vibrant first finger as if drawn towards it by a magnet while the bow swings down on to the string.

A similar technical approach can sometimes be introduced when leaping swiftly to higher accented notes that players find difficult to pitch with certainty. In the Telemann A minor sonata there is a B and a C in the sixth and seventh positions respectively which have to be reached from notes in the lower register. It should be like second nature to find the A with any finger (see p. 22), so if the second or first is placed on it, players should find it relatively easy to strike the B or C above it with the third finger.

A BACKGROUND TO 'TRAC' CONTROL

'Good, you see you were not nervous.' These encouraging words were spoken by Maurice Eisenberg after his initial pupil, a newcomer aged eighteen, had played the first movement of the Boccherini B♭ major concerto at a Master Class at the Cascais International Summer Courses in Portugal. He added quietly, 'Perhaps it might have been still better if you had been a little nervous.' He then proceeded to explain and demonstrate how an inner quickening of the perceptions extending from the mind to the finger tips can enhance and colour a performance and, if well directed, will help to change competence into artistry.

Nervousness, or to use the French expression *trac* which many musicians of diverse countries employ when discussing a problem that knows no geographical boundaries, affects players according to their temperaments. Unless it can be mastered it may ruin a career. Yet those who have never experienced it seldom rise to the greatest heights because it is inherently associated with sensitivity and when controlled, enhances the interpretative vision, leading to increased joy in music-making.

It can come from a variety of causes. Some are psychological, perhaps even transitory, such as the importance of a specific occasion or the presence of a certain person in the audience. Some may be physical: for example a cold can engender a general feeling of heaviness or malaise that affects both the ear and the fingers. It can spring from humility, from a sense that the music is so great that only a supreme artist can hope to capture its true spirit. On the other hand, the excitement of personal association with a deeply felt work, unless compensated by sufficient technical command, may cause fingers and bow to behave unpredictably, giving the effect of carelessness or untidiness.

Experience naturally helps players to overcome such weaknesses. The artist-student soon realizes this when assessing the benefits of a four weeks' master class series at which criticism has to be assimilated immediately in the presence of colleagues and other listeners. These troubles, however, likewise affect players on a more elementary level. It is therefore necessary to consider the question of nervousness on a concrete basis and study it primarily from a technical angle.

On a stringed instrument the adverse effect of *trac* shows itself most frequently in insecurity of the intonation. In many cases this can be attributed to insufficient attention to detail when practising, usually at some point in comparatively early studentship, which breeds, perhaps subconsciously, a feeling of uncertainty. Consequently, as nervousness is akin to fear, when under stress notes and phrases in relatively easy passages are apt to be slightly out of tune and mar an otherwise accomplished performance. At competitions, many a prize has been lost by a spirited contestant to a fellow executant who was more consistent, if less outstanding tonally, because the former failed to maintain the control that the adjudicators considered essential to all-round success.

Most cellists in embryo are taught to locate and make use of three important landmarks: the notes played by the index finger in the first and fourth positions and the harmonics an octave above each open string (see pp. 21–2, 32, and 61). However, this should only be a first step. In order to feel secure students should similarly learn to pitch notes in the intervening positions and half positions. Furthermore, they must train the fingers to move swiftly and surely up and down the string and leap to different notes from any part of the instrument in order to rely upon finding them even when they feel scared.

Practising drills over a drone provided by a lower open string should help to establish confidence in the finger action. This can already be applied when working at simple extensions (see p. 59) and third position vibrato exercises, like:

while many find it advisable to persist in over-string vibrato drills, such as:

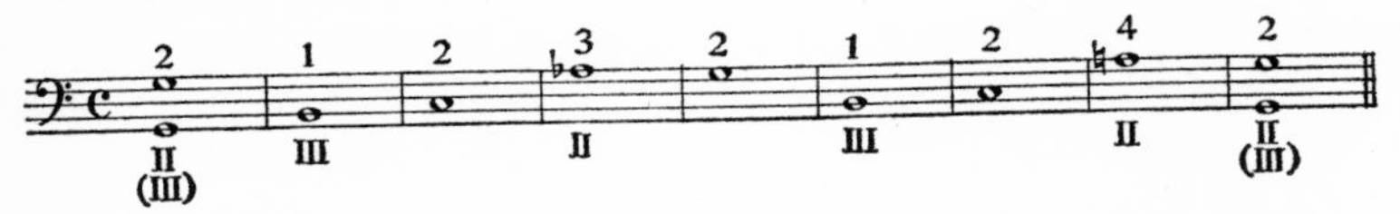

and

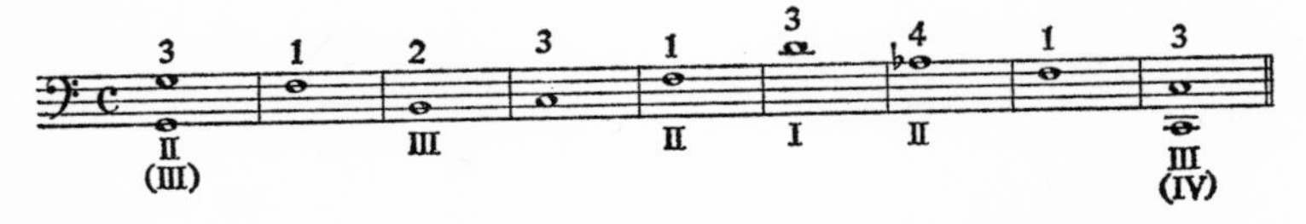

to accustom the finger tips to seek and reach the heart of their notes.

From these modest beginnings, adapted with suitable fingerings to other parts of the instrumental compass, it should be possible to build up an ever-increasing sense of security. More proficient students should include mixed 'one string' arpeggios:

as soon as they are sufficiently at home in the thumb register. These are invaluable because they introduce some awkward shifts and finger placings. They should be practised in all keys, on each string in turn, and beginning up bow as well as down bow.

In preparing works for performance the finger patterns and pointing should be studied until they can be adopted instinctively. Once assimilated they should become a subconscious part of the player's equipment. Eventually this should impose a control that allows the fear of *trac* to be surmounted and turned to excellent account.

PROGRESS

'Progress yesterday is not progress today.' This dictum can be regarded by discriminating players of all grades as both a spur to further effort and a touchstone against complacency.

Change is not necessarily progress although progress can be impeded by ruling out change. Students, nevertheless, must realize that the rising standard of cello playing in the last few decades is enabling even the less gifted among them to take advantage of technical precepts which were formerly considered to be solely suited to advanced performers. This should be encouraged even if at first it seems to lead to a few complications.

For instance, when the 1–2–3 system of fingering (see pp. 111–13) is applied in the fourth position:

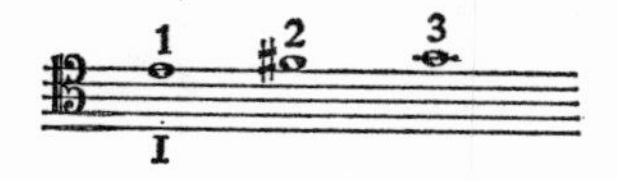

the little finger no longer provides a safe means for pitching a G, C, F or B♭, landmarks on which many aspiring cellists have been accustomed to rely. Players should therefore train themselves as soon as possible to practise shifting to these notes from a lower position and enunciating them with the third finger. In so doing the index finger should be treated as the all-important stepping stone. If it is taught to fall into place by working drills like:

the third finger, when moving directly to the G, should find the heart of its note with ease.

Another fingering device, originally designed for the professional student, can likewise be recommended nowadays to many other players: the substitution of the second for the third finger when a note in the middle register is approached from below in a lyrical passage. The notation plays a decisive part in determining when it should be adopted. For example, if an A immediately above the fourth position occurs in a phrase requiring the prior use of the index finger on F or F♯, the A should be played with the third finger, whereas should the A be preceded by some other note and be followed by one in the lower register, it is usually best to play it in the sixth position with the stronger second finger. The weight of the whole hand falls more naturally on to the second finger so its use has a beneficial effect on the quality and continuity of the tone. This applies on all strings and also to the notes traditionally performed with the third finger in the sixth position. To appreciate its advantages readers can experiment for themselves in an episode in the Fauré *Elégie*:

(from *Elégie*, Fauré)

where the climax occurs on the C string, listening critically to the sonority.

However the main difference between the technical requirements of today's average amateur cellist and those in the first quarter of the century lies in the role of the left hand in the top registers. This trend has become increasingly apparent owing to the ever-growing demands of forward-thinking composers. Furthermore, while this 'new music' was formerly only attempted by the most proficient players, others, drawn from the rank and file, now strive to emulate them.

Thus once the hand has been taught to master the problems of simple thumb position, students of every calibre should start working at advanced technique. The ability to balance and control the hand in every part of the highest register should be a major objective, whether the thumb is in its 'closed' placing, a tone or a semitone behind the first finger, or separated from it by the space of a far larger interval. Exercises made up of ascending and descending scale passages in unisons and tenths:

and

should be attempted by all ambitious cellists, in addition to drills on the lines of those quoted on pages 33 and 34.

It is equally important to develop the thumb action so that it can move freely on its own while the fingers continue to vibrate their notes or execute complicated figures higher up the fingerboard. Students with sufficient experience should make up exercises founded on the notes of an open chord covering all four strings:

vibrating as freely as possible, especially on the higher strings.

At performance the hand may be called upon to assume a number of widely divergent placings in the upper register with little opportunity for preparation. Cellists should consequently strive to increase their instrumental vocabularies by learning to approach intervals of all kinds direct from the neck positions. As a preliminary measure, drills built on four notes an octave apart on different strings, say:

can be recommended. Always keep the thumb firmly on the string once it has been placed on its note. Then short exercises in double stopping which alternate constantly between the two registers:

with different fingerings on the top note, should be incorporated. Be sure to return the thumb to its 'home base' behind the neck of the cello opposite the second finger when playing the sixths and the fourth in the lower register.

VARIETY IN VIBRATO

A fine, flexible vibrato, adaptable for use on all strings and in every position is vital to interpretation on the cello and its importance cannot be overrated. It is subject to the utmost variety of treatment, affecting specifically the speed, width, and intensity of the oscillations. Few players, no matter how gifted they may be, can associate themselves solely by instinct with all the shadings involved: while certain types of vibrato may be temperamentally akin to them considerable thought and study are generally required before this inborn facility can be expanded to cover the full gamut of mood and nuance inherent in the music. It is an over-simplification to regard vibrato purely as a natural asset or a hallmark of talent.

Advice on elementary vibrato drills has already been given. (See pp. 17–19.) Attention will therefore be focused here on rather less concrete aspects of the question. Although the player may not always realize it, vibrato has its source in the 'motor power' generated in the instrumentalist's mind and imagination. From there its impetus is carried subconsciously from behind the shoulder-blade, down the left arm into the finger tip and so on to the string.

Its action is centred in the finger singing its note, but every part of the arm and hand unit from the elbow onwards shares responsibility for it to some extent. Of these 'supporting factors', perhaps the most important—albeit frequently neglected because it is the least obvious—is the thumb. It should vibrate with the fingers whether the hand is in the lower registers or the highest ranges of thumb position, respectively either loosely touching the neck of the cello or pinning the string to the fingerboard.

Some cellists vibrate too quickly: they need to become less hectic. Others cause the tone to sound sluggish by constant use of a very slow oscillation: these should quicken their vibrations. Many beginners are scared, thinking that a free vibrato will upset the intonation, which it should not do if the finger tip is taught to sink into the heart of its note. (See p. 119.) Such students are apt to stop the oscillations after each note instead of employing them with a sense of continuity, following the melodic line and according to the phrasing. This tendency, if unchecked, engenders a disturbing mannerism that can be difficult to eradicate.

The basic oscillation should be neither too wide nor too narrow: a medium rate should be sought and established from the first. It should vary somewhat according to the register on the principle that a slower, broader movement can be advocated for the 'neck' positions, particularly on the lower, thicker strings, whereas the vibrations should be slightly quickened and contracted as the hand moves towards the bridge. Upon this 'normal' vibrato every possible change of pace and intensity should eventually be superimposed according to the colour scheme and dynamics of each composition. In performance such adjustments may have to be made more than once while drawing a single stroke of the bow.

In lyrical works the bowing usually acts in sympathy with the vibrato, but in rapid passages the left hand is frequently called upon to maintain a vibrant background while the bow executes rhythmic or percussive feats. In accentuation both hands are equal partners: for instance in the main theme of Saint-Saëns's *Allegro Appassionato*:

(from *Allegro Appassionato,* Saint-Saëns)

the accents should be made by reinforcing the vibrato at the precise moment that the bow strikes the string, the speed of the bow being reduced immediately afterwards while the oscillations become correspondingly smaller.

Originally the primary function of vibrato was to add lustre to the tone. This remains one of its major objectives, especially in cello music written before the nineteenth century. In those days the Church, the court, and the stage were the chief sources of creative opportunities for the composer. To match the spirit of this more leisured age the vibrato, in general, can be more measured than might be appropriate in compositions of a later date. Yet even within these limits something more may be needed. Take Kodály's setting for cello and piano of Bach's Choral Preludes and consider the diversity of vibrato techniques required in order to play them convincingly. The colours range from the other-worldly aestheticism of the first prelude where vibrato can be eliminated to the tragic resignation implicit in the final phrase of the third, marked '*con summa espressione de dolore e lutto*'.

Beethoven's sonatas opened a new vista for cellists. Schumann, Brahms, Dvořák, and many others added to it as the Romantic age progressed. Throughout its course the need for a more flexible approach to vibrato was coming increasingly to the fore. This trend was further stimulated by the influence of the Impressionist school. Nearer our own day noted masters from Central and Eastern Europe, such as Bloch, Kodály, Martinů, and Prokofiev, benefited by the widening instrumental horizons to link the glowing virility of the cello, which was reflected by something in their personal outlooks, with exciting experiments in the idioms of their countries and their times.

One word of warning. Vibrato, which has been evolved to enhance musical performance, must never be allowed to detract from its success through clumsy handling. For example, it must never be permitted to interfere with the strength and clarity of the articulation. In pieces that are both lyrical and rhythmic like Fauré's *Sicilienne* the enunciation should be effected by the vibrant finger descending firmly on to the string. Players should aim at differentiating between the many shades and styles of vibrato suited to divers works and epochs. Wise cellists know that it is through a finely tempered vibrato that they are best able to make their interpretations a living experience.

POSTLUDE

The Master Speaks

EVER SINCE Casals's first appearance, the reasons for his supremacy have been debated by cellists ranging from his older colleagues of the late nineteenth century, to most of whom his ideas were completely revolutionary, to players who are about to emerge today, having been educated to profit from the effects of his innovations.

Some of the latter are apt to refer to his unique standing with a touch of incredulity. Can it be true, or is there a Casals legend? They have probably learnt to associate his name with such concrete advantages as instrumental balance, finger percussion, double extensions, the ability to bow freely without exaggeration of movement, and 'expressive intonation'. But they attend concerts featuring other renowned cellists who give accomplished performances of taxing compositions, and may perhaps wonder what it is that supposedly set him apart. Scepticism was also said to exist, albeit for a different reason, at the outset of his career. For more than a decade after his debut nearly all his co-instrumentalists considered both his interpretations and his technique as something personal, to be admired but not to be copied.

The majority of players in the intervening years, however, could not content themselves without probing further. Casals had proved that talent, logic, and determination had enabled him to find the means to make the once cumbersome cello sound as easy to handle as the violin. It became increasingly evident to thinking cellists that many time-honoured ideas from former years should be superseded by something more flexible and far-reaching which could ultimately be made accessible, at least to a certain degree, to all who could master their often exacting basic principles.

Meanwhile Casals, however, published nothing about his 'method'. He approved of Alexanien's and Eisenberg's books both publicly in his forewords and privately in conversation. Yet except for such warm endorsements he remained silent about his own attitude towards teaching. Apart from a relatively few private lessons his direct contribution to the pedagogic world comes solely through his Master Classes and his orchestral rehearsals. Partly on this account many may have come to regard his personality as something of an enigma.

Strangely enough it took what was intended as a laudatory comment in the United States press following the presentation of the Freedom Award to make him speak. The occasion was an informal gathering of a few friends at the Casals's hotel in New York.

'Have you seen the papers?' he asked. 'Imagine, they call me a great cellist!' The faces around him were blank: there seemed nothing unusual in that. 'I am not a cellist,' he continued. 'I am a musician. That is much more important! Can you believe it?' he repeated to drive in his point. 'They keep referring to me as a cellist instead of as a musician!'

Although everyone present was familiar with his ideology and achievements, his words left a deep impression. They offered irrefutable evidence of the motive power that had driven him to find the means to rise to the heights on his chosen instrument. From the beginning it was his insistence of interpreting the music completely and uncompromisingly as it was revealed to him through the study of the score and the history of the composer, that had forced him to discover and perfect a way through which this vision could be expressed impeccably on the cello. Without instrumental control of the highest order he could never have brought the great masterpieces to life according to his own standards: without exceptional talent it would have been equally impossible for him to have accomplished his purpose.

Recognizing the enormity of this task, the result of which has elevated the whole level of cello playing, it is hardly surprising if today most experts regard it as the summit of his attainments. The reminder that, to him, it was a secondary goal is therefore a timely warning. Those who would profit by his example should bear in mind that in his estimation, before all else comes the music with its purity of style, shapeliness, profundity, and colour, its graciousness, dynamism, and warmth, and the subtlety that lies behind each phrase, no matter how familiar.

INDEX